The JOY
of the
Quickie

KATE STEVENS More Than

150 Ways to
Do It *NOW!*

Adamsmedia

AVON, MASSACHUSETTS

Published by
Adams Media, a division of F+W Media, Inc.
57 Littlefield Street, Avon, MA 02322. U.S.A.
www.adamsmedia.com

Previously published as *Instant Gratification* by Kate Stevens, copyright © 2009 by
F+W Media, Inc., ISBN 10: 1-60550-156-5, ISBN 13: 978-1-60550-156-7.

ISBN 10: 1-4405-2788-1
ISBN 13: 978-1-4405-2788-3
eISBN 10: 1-4405-2813-6
eISBN 13: 978-1-4405-2813-2

Printed in the United States of America.

10   9   8   7   6   5   4   3   2   1

Library of Congress Cataloging-in-Publication Data
is available from the publisher.

This book is available at quantity discounts for bulk purchases.
For information, please call 1-800-289-0963.

Contents

Introduction

In the world of sex, the "quickie" is like a fun size candy bar you pop into your mouth for an instant burst of feel-good satisfaction. Quickies cut to the chase, get to the point, and deliver what you want when you want it. The only tricky part is "Where can I have it?" because the urge for a quickie can take hold in the most unlikely places—but fear not! This handy guide is here to make matters easy. With a little preparation and imagination, your love life will truly live up to the promise of "anytime, anywhere."

Listen, anybody can have sex in a bed. So predictable, so routine! Once you extend the field of possibilities to elevators, corn mazes, pickup trucks, and yes, even rodeos, bowling alleys, and walk-in freezers, sex becomes an opportunity that pops up everywhere you look! The element of danger is sure to spice up the sex, and what's more, afterward you'll have stories to tell your closest friends and, years from now, yarns to spin for your grandchildren, who will be astounded not only that you had sex but also that you did it in a hot air balloon.

More than 150 possible locations are listed alphabetically, from "AA meeting" to "Zoo." Each entry lays the groundwork with a description of the situation, assesses the dangers involved, and advises you on the best logistics and strategies to pull things off (so to speak). If you've never contemplated getting it on in a canoe, a drive-thru, a family reunion, or a pumpkin patch, you'll need to pay close attention to special considerations and advice listed in each entry.

The Joy of the Quickie gives you everything you need to strike while the iron is hot. Good sex may be worth waiting for, but often the best sex is the kind you just gotta have NOW, no matter where you are or what you're doing (or even who you're with)!

Read on, make your plans, and enjoy sex this instant!

AA Meeting

You've admitted you have a problem, but now the problem is, twelve steps feels like eleven too many! Is that hottie across the sharing circle winking at you?

Risk Factor: 5

If you get caught, you may be asked to take it down the hall to the Sex Addicts Anonymous.

DO IT (NOW):

While listening to people's stories, take note of emotional stability, so you can make the best choice. (Forget the group moderators: pesky "ethics" rules them out.) Next, scope your location during coffee break: if you're in a church basement, look for a private confessional room; in a Knights of Columbus hall, look for the broom closet. Wait until the end of the meeting to put a cherry on top of an evening of catharsis. Consider stretching out the four bases into twelve steps, the first step being a comforting hug enhanced with a fast feel. As you build trust, move on to kissing. Use your imagination to fill in the rest, but don't lose sight of your primary purpose in attending the AA meeting.

Considerations:

If you get caught, use your alcoholism as an excuse ("I couldn't help myself—and at least I'm not drinking!").

Airplane

Traveling by airplane can be boring and nerve-wracking. What better way to pass the time and release some stress than by joining the mile-high club. Get out of your seat and head to the lavatory for fun.

Risk Factor: 2

A few things could make this tryst a little dangerous. The bathrooms on airplanes are small, so be prepared to get creative! Also, remember that even over the roar of the engine, passengers and flight attendants might hear you.

DO IT (NOW):

Pretend you aren't feeling well and ask your partner to help you to the bathroom. That way, suspicions won't be raised if noises are heard or if you're in there too long. There's not much room for a lot of movement, so the best position is from behind with the woman bent over the toilet. If she's wearing a skirt there's no need to strip—men can just unzip. If anyone walks in on you, she can act like she was getting sick, especially if he's holding onto her hair. Keep in mind that turbulence can work in your favor, so plan your bathroom trip for when the ride gets bumpy!

Considerations:

People that need to use the bathroom and are waiting in line might get impatient and call the flight attendant.

Airport

Never has the sentence "I had a layover in Atlanta" carried so much weight. You're either stuck in a strange city for the night or delayed for what feels like an eternity, and nothing would calm your nerves more than having someone fly you to the moon.

Risk Factor: 3

Choose wisely, and remember that federal agents often go undercover. You don't want someone yelling "Terrorist!" when all you want to do is hide something in a body cavity!

DO IT (NOW):

Keep your tryst out of the airport bathroom: many a politician and rock star has been disgraced this way. Instead, approach your hook-up and suggest you both give up your seats on this flight to get an overnight stay at a local hotel. Airports also have bars, full of stressed-out businesspeople and young hotties gearing up for fun in Cancun. Ladies, try the pickup line: "I'm worried my underwire bra will set off the metal detector. Care to help me get it off?" And for the gents: "I know about a perk you won't find in first class." If you're rebuffed, say you'll toss in a free bag of peanuts.

Considerations:

Time your tryst wisely. Otherwise, you may end up running through the terminal to make your connection with your pants around your ankles.

Location 4:

Alley

You're in the city with no money for a hotel room. Fortunately, the alley behind the hotel affords some privacy! Suggest to your hook-up that you take a shortcut—and what is a quickie but a quick cut to the chase?

Risk Factor: 2

Anyone who happens upon you and your hook-up is not going to act surprised: it's an alley, after all. Chances are, anyone who passes by will just keep on walking.

DO IT (NOW):

The longer, the better—and I'm talking about the alley here, silly goose. Longer alleys tend to be darker alleys, and waiting till nighttime will grant you cover. If someone goes so far as to flash a light in your direction, say, "Hey, do you mind? I'm trying to save my marriage here!" (Hearing this from the female will put anyone's fear of public assault to rest.) The alley may be a bit smelly or dirty, so pour a bottle of your favorite cologne onto the pavement in a circle around where you plan your quickie: that'll stave off any other scent long enough to make the quickie an olfactory pleasure.

Considerations:

As with all public sex, you run the risk of police intervention, especially if that old lady peeking out her window doesn't like what she sees!

Location 5:

Ambulance

The urge for a quickie often feels like a life or death emergency, so where better to satisfy oneself than an ambulance? You'll be surrounded by equipment engineered to cure what ails you.

Risk Factor: 2

If anything, the penalty for having sex in an ambulance is being trucked off to the branch of the psycho ward where they deal with sexual pathology.

DO IT (NOW):

If you find yourself in an ambulance for a genuine medical emergency, hitting on the EMT isn't going to be top of mind. Instead, start dating an EMT. Once you have your hooks in one, see if your lover can arrange a rendezvous. Sex in a parked ambulance doesn't have the same charge as speeding through traffic, sirens blaring, while you and your lover are inching toward climax, but with imagination, you can recreate that sense of urgency that accelerates your orgasmic response. If you're playing patient, pretend that mouth-to-mouth resuscitation and a vigorous chest massage has yielded no results, and it's time for more desperate measures!

Considerations:

Once you're over the novelty of ambulance sex, dump the EMT. Don't worry: they're used to losing people.

Apple Picking

According to the Bible, the first sex happened as a result of an apple. So there's something exciting about doing it amid the rustle of leaves and the smell of fallen fruit. You can almost hear someone whispering from the tree branches above you to go for it.

Risk Factor: 3

The problem with apple orchards (aside from being public, opening you to charges of indecency) is the number of sharp and sticky objects they contain. Difficulties range from getting poked by branches to stepping or lying on a rotten apple— which can really kill the mood.

DO IT (NOW):

Find a secluded corner of the orchard, far away from families, especially those with loud, annoying kids. Fortunately, apple trees grow thick and block out a lot of sight lines. The woman sits on a low branch, while the man stands in front of her, gradually easing her off the branch so she's leaning on it but no longer sitting on it. For further support, she can grip the branch above her. Jeans and tee shirts are okay, but be prepared to zip up fast if you hear someone approaching.

Considerations:

Hay rides taking apple pickers between the rows of trees.

Aquarium

Studying the motion of the ocean has you thinking about rocking your raft. Birds do it, bees do it, and even baby Beluga whales do it, so take a break from the seal show for a quick treat.

Risk Factor: 5

Aquariums are big with families, so there may be plenty of children around. Be discreet, be quick, and if you must make noise, try squealing like a dolphin: *Eeek! Eeek! Eeek! Flipper? I hardly knew her!*

DO IT (NOW):

When you've found a private stairwell or penguin shower stall, go with the theme and make your quickie aquatic. One of you plays the trainer, while the other plays the sea creature. Be sure you have a bag of Swedish fish candies to use as rewards for small tricks: clapping, kissing the tip of a body part, doing a waddle dance, and showing how long you can hold your breath while engaged in other activities. Another wet dream to fulfill would be "The Mermaid Who Grants Wishes."

Considerations:

Surrounded as you are by the smell of fish, no one will ever suspect.

ATM Vestibule

Money and sex. They go together like . . . bread and butter. Like death and taxes. Like guns and roses. The very openness of ATMs gives you a chance for an extra thrill. This is your chance to go really public and make a really meaningful deposit.

Risk Factor: 4

There's no question of your getting noticed. You will. ATMs have cameras trained on them twenty-four hours a day. You have to accept that as one of the challenges and go with it.

DO IT (NOW):

ATM vestibules are either out in the open or behind glass doors, giving access only with an ATM card. The latter are better for your purposes, since they offer a tiny measure of privacy. The key here is to be fast and to do it late at night, when there aren't many people around. Since the cameras are generally located above the machines and since you're going to be photographed no matter what you do, you can give the security system a thrill. The woman leans back against the machine, while the man enters her. Loose clothing is a necessity. For an extra fillip, blow a kiss to the camera before leaving.

Considerations:

Bank robbers.

Attic

In the summertime, the attic is a bit musty, the place where you stored that box of pictures that Aunt Reynalda gave you of old family reunions. But in the winter, with snow coming down outside and a few candles scattered here and there to shed a golden light over the bundles and boxes, it's a mysterious and romantic place to enjoy one another.

Risk Factor: 1

It's unlikely you'll run into any problems, since it's your own house (at least, we presume so) and you've got plenty of privacy. About the only problem is the dust that tends to accumulate, and since there's nothing sexy about asthma masks, you might want to give the place a quick going over with a broom before doing anything.

DO IT (NOW):

Summer makes attics hot and stuffy, so that's probably not the best time to try things. Much better is an early winter or late fall night, when the weather's started to turn cool. You can bring along a couple of blankets for warmth, and some candles and a few sticks of incense for atmosphere. Since attics are associated with old photo albums, you might even want to take along a camera and create some sexy memories of the occasion.

Considerations:

Spiders, beetles, and nesting pigeons.

Location 10:

Ballet

Your partner is not so hot on a night at the ballet, but the promise of a potential quickie (in dance terms, *lay de deux*) makes it *much* more appealing.

Risk Factor: 2

Ballets are typically held in large performance centers, with stairwells and uninhabited corners. Few go to the ballet to have sex, which means no one will expect you to do so!

DO IT (NOW):

Explore the hall by looking around during intermission. While watching the ballet itself, gentlemen take note of how gracefully the dancers lift their female counterparts by placing their hands beneath the rib cage, and ladies, take note of the male dancers' fabulous packages. Dance is basically a way for two people to have sex with their clothes on. Whisper suggestions to your partner throughout: other people will think you're a critic. Wait for an act to finish before you head to your hook-up spot. The fact that you're gussied up will make undressing all the more sexy. If discovered, simply say, "Do you mind? We're in the middle of a performance!"

Considerations:

Ballet is good instruction for sex: to be light on your feet, to be mindful of every movement, and to keep your legs strong.

Bank

Perhaps the gentleman is interested in making a deposit? Or the lady will do anything to get her loan approved? With so much money around, no wonder your lust is stirred!

Risk Factor: 4

Perils here include being locked in a safe overnight or, more plausibly, being caught on tape by any one of a thousand hidden security cameras. Security may interpret your escapades as a distraction for an imminent robbery attempt. So take care, Bonnie and Clyde.

DO IT (NOW):

Your best bet here is to tell the bankers you're interested in purchasing a safe deposit box. Then you have a reason to be left alone in a room with some privacy. So come back with your lover and tell the manager you'd like to "put something in your box" and that you may need a little time. You and your lover may still be caught on camera, but such are the voyeuristic pleasures of high-risk quickies. The manager will likely wait until you are finished, then cordially ask you to take your box elsewhere...like a mattress at home.

Considerations:

It's a perfect time for the guy to say, "This is a stickup!" and for the gal to respond, "It certainly is!"

Location 12:

Baseball Park

Time for the boys (and girls) of summer to round the bases and score one for the home team. After all, this is America's pastime. (We're talking about baseball, right?)

Risk Factor: 2

Half of the people at the game are drunk, to begin with. And then you have the people in the stands. Aberrant behavior may be penalized, but it's also somewhat expected.

DO IT (NOW):

Attending a night game will at least give you the cover of darkness as protection against snoopers. You have two opportunities to steal away: (1) when the game really gets exciting, which may be a long wait; or (2) the seventh-inning stretch. Most of the attention in the park will be focused between the pitcher and the batter, so see if you can find a spot behind the left field wall. While the people in the stands are hollering "We need a pitcher, not a belly itcher," you and your lover will be singing "I need me some nookie, not a traded rookie." Or, if you like, make the phrase "I could use a belly itcher right about now" your code for a midgame tryst.

Considerations:

Watch out for breaking balls and wild pitches.

Bathtub

Warm water. Scented candles. Bath salts. And you and your partner wrapped in a cocoon of soapy goodness. There's nothing quite like sex in a bathtub. And, conveniently, you've already got your clothes off.

Risk Factor: 1

Really, there's not much that can happen to you. Even if you slip underwater for a moment, your partner is right there to help you out. The biggest risk is getting soap in your eyes.

DO IT (NOW):

The real trick is choosing a bathtub that's big enough. The best ones are Jacuzzi tubs, where the streams of bubbles can add considerably to your enjoyment. Failing that, maybe you'll be lucky enough to get one of those old-fashioned ball-and-claw-foot cast-iron tubs, the kind your great-grandparents had in their bathroom. The missionary position doesn't work very well here. The best way is to sit facing one another. The woman wraps her legs around the man's waist, and you hold one another steady while moving gently so as not to splash water over the sides of the tub. Don't fill the tub too full, and remember to get rid of any rubber duckies that may be lying around.

Considerations:

Nosy children who suddenly "need" to use the bathroom.

Location 14:

Beach

Hot sand, sweaty bodies, skimpy clothing, a sunny day—how can you *not* want to have sex when you're on the beach? Being around so many near-nude bodies is a total turn-on.

Risk Factor: 5

People expect sexual behavior on the beach, so lifeguards will be on the lookout. With so many kids around, anyone who catches you is sure to be bent out of shape.

DO IT (NOW):

I know what you're thinking: "We'll just put a towel over ourselves." Um, no. Discreet, that ain't. A far safer strategy is to bring a tent (not see-through) and anchor it so that a stiff wind won't blow it away. When you're inside, be quiet or risk drawing attention. Most folks clear off the beach at sunset, so you buy yourself a little more privacy with good timing. Bring a sweatshirt to put on after any naked escapades, because without the sun, the beach can get pretty chilly. The perfect time is when the beach is totally abandoned late at night and you can barely see your hand in front of your face. In that case, lay out the blanket and indulge to your heart's content!

Considerations:

Sand has a talent for finding its way into the damnedest places on your body.

Location 15:

Bell Tower

After a long climb to the top of a bell tower, you realize that you and your lover are all alone. The bell chimes and the vibrations flow through both of your bodies and suddenly you can't control yourselves.

Risk Factor: 2

The damage to your eardrums from the loud bell might be the only danger standing between you and a good time. Also beware of vertigo . . . just don't look down. Hopefully you'll be in the throes of passion before a fear of heights sets in.

DO IT (NOW):

Bell towers are usually tight quarters, plus you have the swinging bell to worry about. Time your fling right so you get down to business before the hour strikes. If there are no other people around you can lay yourself down on the floor or if you don't have a fear of heights, bend over the side. You'll be able to keep a lookout. If you hear someone climbing the bell tower, you should have enough time to readjust clothing, etc. before they reach the top.

Considerations:

Before you make your bell tower trip, rent *9½ Weeks* or *Mermaids*. Both of them have sexy bell tower scenes and you might get a few tips.

Biker Bar

You're in the mood for your lover to call you "Easy Rider" by the end of the night, and you've mustered up the courage to hit the local biker bar. It's leather, studs, jeans, bandanas, and tattoos all the way!

Risk Factor: 1

Bikers may look like a tough crowd, but most are just rebels who don't care for phonies, wannabes, hangers-on, or prudes. If you be yourself and buy 'em a couple of rounds, you stand a better chance of being declared okay.

DO IT (NOW):

Both the guy and the gal should wear leather chaps, which, in addition to serving a biker function, give you easy access to naughty parts. Guys, don't try to out-tough the tough guys. Gals, now is the time and place to show you're a good sport—a pat on the ass should be considered a compliment! (They're bikers, for crissake.) And feel free to ask your new biker friends where the best place is to score a quickie. A few of the bigger bikers may agree to stand around the bar booth while you and your lover get your motors running. If the price is letting a couple of 'em watch, play along. Buy another round of shots.

Considerations:

Don't tell them you arrived at the bar in a minivan or anything that was made in Japan.

Bookstore

You're strolling through the racks and stumble on the sex section. You pick up a copy of the Kama Sutra and think "can I bend my legs like that?" You came to pick up a light beach read but you decide to have a quickie instead.

Risk Factor: 3

Highly dangerous! They say nobody reads anymore, but it's not true. There will be people everywhere. Remember to steer clear of the children's section where there is sure to be plenty of little ones running around.

DO IT (NOW):

The safe and boring thing to do is take a quick trip to the bathroom. If you want to really take a risk you'll find a section of the store with the least amount of traffic to get busy in. Try the gardening section. Really, any place with dark corners or tall obstructing bookshelves will do.

Considerations:

If you get cold feet, you can always pick up a copy of *The Joy of Sex* to enjoy with your partner in the privacy of your home!

Location 18:

Bowling Alley

Bowling, as we all know, takes balls. And so does grabbing a quickie between frames. Sex, however, may be the highest score you have in a bowling alley, so break out your gutter balls and aim for the split.

Risk Factor: 5

Bowling alleys are terrific places for double entendres and flirting, but since every lane is out in the open, there aren't many places to indulge in some nookie. Alleys are also popular for kids' parties, and an angry parent may call a lawyer instead of the cops.

DO IT (NOW):

Find a bowling alley that has "night bowling" or "rock and roll night," where the lights are dim and afford you some cover. Go with a group, so your lane is not conspicuously empty during your quickie. Also, while friends are bowling, you and your partner may be able to squeeze in a few fast feels. Bathrooms may be too busy, so scope out the back of the building: it may back up to an empty lot, the woods, or a similarly private space. Bowling shoes don't have much traction, so have stand-up sex at your own risk!

Considerations:

Some bowling alleys let you purchase a memento bowling pin, which can serve double duty as an athletic dildo. (More comfy than using a trophy!)

Boxing Ring

In this corner, measuring 36-24-36, the Fiery Fornicator—The Lady! And in this corner, measuring 7 inches when fully aroused, the Sheik of the Sheets—The Gentleman! Now, listen you two, I want a good, dirty quickie. All blows below the belt.

Risk Factor: 3

Depending on how rough you like it, you might get a few bruises, if not your heart broken. When you go down (on your partner) for the count, muster the strength to get up and keep it up.

DO IT (NOW):

If you're friends with stadium security and can sneak into the ring the night before the fight, go a single round and be on your way. A more homey strategy is to block out some space in your house or apartment, put a stool in opposite corners, and play some pumped-up tunes while you and your opponent go head to head. Only playful jabs and goosing grabs allowed. Dance around one another and build up the foreplay energy, then lock horns and make contact. Don't wait for the referee to separate you, because there is no ref.

Considerations:

Only throw in the towel when you need something to wipe yourself with.

Location 20:

Bridge

You're walking with your lover along a lovely bridge overlooking a moonlight river. As you pass over, you remind your partner that there's a toll to pay, and it doesn't involve money.

Risk Factor: 1

No one hangs out by a bridge: they're places of transit, with cars in a hurry to get to their destination. You're relatively safe here from discovery, especially if it's closed for repair.

DO IT (NOW):

First, have the quickie *beneath* the bridge. The underside of bridges, be warned, are not known for their cleanliness. You're likely to discover detritus and litter, even broken bottles or a shopping cart. If there's no clear spot to lay down on, go for the stand-up quickie, and remember: there's a big echo under the bridge, so any loud noises you make are likely to disturb a family of pigeons. But the rumbling of cars passing overhead may give you some good vibrations!

Considerations:

Depending on the construction of the bridge, gaining access to its underbelly may involve some steep climbing, so be sure to wear appropriate footwear.

Bus

Ralph Cramden of *The Honeymooners* may not have been the most romantic of husbands ("One of these days, Alice! *Pow!* To the moon!"), but as a city bus driver, he surely must have been aware of the possibilities of making love in the back of a bus. Make your way to the rear, find a secluded seat, and think of Ralph and Alice.

Risk Factor: 3

Buses may not be as smelly and unpleasant as they were twenty years ago, but they're still public. Chances of being exposed by passengers remain high, and being put off the bus while pulling up your clothing is humiliating. You also might end up in the middle of nowhere.

DO IT (NOW):

The best possibilities are offered by intercity buses (Greyhound, Trailways, and so on). The trip will give you plenty of time, and the seats are usually high-backed, which should shield you from curious onlookers. The most subtle way to success lies in the realm of oral sex. If the woman puts her head down to rest on the man's lap, and no one is looking your way, there's nothing to stop some discreet enjoyment. If you want to indulge in anything more energetic, it's best to do so when there aren't many people on the bus and when most of them are sitting toward the front, away from you.

Considerations:

Old chewing gum stuck to the seat.

Location 22:

Bushes

You're out for a romantic walk in a pristine countryside. The sun is shining, birds are singing, romance is in the air. And off to one side of the path is a handy clump of bushes that will shield you from prying eyes. Quickly you slip out of sight and let the games begin.

Risk Factor: 1

As long as you're careful about the bushes you choose and avoid anything with prickles, there really isn't any danger. The chance of someone seeing you is minimal, and if they do they're the ones who are intruding.

DO IT (NOW):

The key here is in the selection of bushes. Don't try anything in the holly, blackberry, roses, or gorse: there's nothing more calculated to kill the mood. Something soft and pliant is best, since you don't want small branches sticking you in awkward places. Make sure they're tall enough to hide you, even if one of you is sitting astride the other. Some minimal protective clothing is advisable unless you plan to use a blanket. Amid everything else, keep an ear peeled for passersby.

Considerations:

Beetles, ants, and irritated birds.

Location 23:

Canoe

You and your friends have ventured to the river for a little summer debauchery. Your cooler is packed, and you're ready for a day of floating and fun. Eight beers in, your paddle partner starts looking really good.

Risk Factor: 3

Vigorous motion can easily capsize a canoe, so make sure you can swim. Also, check the little seats and cubbies for poisonous spiders. No one wants that kind of love bite.

DO IT (NOW):

This is a family environment, so the best approach is to make the guy invisible. Have him lay down lengthwise in the bottom of the boat. Strip off your life vests and place them in the bottom of the canoe—one under his head (for comfort) and one under his hips (for leverage). The woman can easily straddle him, using the crossbars to facilitate north-south movement. Keep a paddle close by to fake downstream progress if a raft full of children passes by.

Considerations:

Mosquito bites and postcoital attachment.

Location 24:

Car Show

The car—especially if it's red, shiny, and fast—has been called the ultimate American sex symbol. At most car shows, the level of testosterone is right up there with a Sylvester Stallone film festival. So why not give in, find somewhere private, and give expression to all that energy and hotness?

Risk Factor: 1

There are plenty of places at a car show where you're unlikely to be disturbed, at least for a couple of minutes. In any case, even if you're found out you're more likely to be applauded than censured.

DO IT (NOW):

The ultimate high at a car show would be to do it in one of the cars on display—say, a Lamborghini or a Ferrari. Unfortunately, the cars tend to be heavily guarded, so your easiest course of action is to find a private room or closet somewhere off the main showroom. To get in the mood, walk the showroom floor for a while, admiring the long, sleek, sexy lines of the Jaguars, Lexuses, and Corvettes. If possible, stroke the hood ornaments. Then slip into a closet for some private enjoyment.

Considerations:

Busybody maintenance workers looking for a pail and a mop.

Car Wash

It's slow, it's dark, and it's wet. The automatic drive-through car wash is one of the best places to be bad.

Risk Factor: 1

Not a lot of danger here, except the usual danger when doing it in the car. Cramped spaces, accidental gear changes, and the occasional horn honk. With all of the high-powered jets and soapy foam covering the windows, no one will know what you are up to for the next 3 or 4 minutes. Make it quick though. By the time the dry cycle arrives, your fun will be over.

DO IT (NOW):

Time is your enemy so prepare ahead of time. Ladies, wear a skirt with no panties. Men, unzip that fly before the car gets on the track. As soon as the car wash attendant is out of view, you're in the clear. The straddle is your best bet here. If the woman is driving she can just straddle the man in the passenger seat. She won't have the steering wheel in her back and the man can watch to make sure she's back in her spot by the time the ride is over.

Considerations:

If you're not careful, the inside of your car might also need a wash afterwards.

Casino

Whether you're on your last chip or have just beat the house, you're in a risk-taking mood, and you're not alone: the place is crawling with high rollers, low ballers, and, one hopes, addicts desperate for a piece of the action.

Risk Factor: 1

Most casinos are attached to a hotel, which makes stealing away an easy bet. Hitting the casino midday during the week guarantees you'll only find seniors who got there by bus.

DO IT (NOW):

A gamble is basically a dare with something riding on it, so use the atmosphere to your advantage. Your willingness to get laid is the safest bet in the entire house! Trade a blow job for a chip. If the roulette wheel lands on red, she's on top; if it lands on black, he enjoys the privilege. If your partner is on a losing streak, whisper in his or her ear that the table may have "gone cold," but you're hot, and the next token in your slot will score three cherries in a row. A casino is ripe with flirtatious double entendres, so enjoy! You or your lover may lose the kitty, but there's always plenty of pussy to pull toward you with both hands!

Considerations:

Don't let the gambling spirit of throwing caution to the wind make you careless with your quickie. Remember discretion and protection.

Casket

Sex and death are unlikely but historic partners, and if a little morbidity reminds you to live life to the fullest, where's the harm? There's a whole Goth vampire vibe to doing it in a coffin.

Risk Factor: 3

Relax: There's no danger of being trapped and subsequently buried alive after having had sex in a casket. (But what a way to go!)

DO IT (NOW):

Access to caskets is made through funeral homes, which have models on display. There are caskets built to accommodate two people, and it wouldn't be the first time for funeral home directors to hear that you and your partner would like to get inside to test it out for size. Still, two able-bodied people in the prime of life showing up at a funeral home may arouse suspicion, especially if you ask to be shut into the casket and left alone for seven minutes. Solution? (1) Pay off the funeral home director; (2) date a funeral home director; or (3) buy the casket and have it delivered to your home.

Considerations:

Opt for comfort. Sex in a plain pine box is nothing to write home about.

Cave

In *Young Frankenstein,* Madeleine Kahn got it on with the Creature in a cave. Six times. Why not follow their example. Some caves may be dank and creepy, but others are magical places. Find a nice dark nook, spread out a wooly blanket, and get busy.

Risk Factor: 2

Unless you're trying something in Carlsbad Caverns, most caves are private sorts of places, so the risk of exposure is limited. You're more apt to have a problem with stony ground or banging your head against a low ceiling, but with reasonable care you should be able to avoid either of those problems.

DO IT (NOW):

Not many caves are big enough to stand up in, but even one that you can comfortably sit up in is fine. Choose a spot far enough away from the entrance to avoid discovery but close enough that you're still near the light. For extra light, bring along a couple of candles or a lantern. Since the ground is probably rock or stone, supply yourself with a couple of blankets. Caves are almost always chillier than the air outside, so wear warm but comfortable clothes that you can shed under the blankets.

Considerations:

Bats. Swooping bats. Lots of them.

Cemetery

There's something about death and sex. Maybe it's a reminder of our own mortality. Or maybe you just think vampires are sexy as hell. As the sun sets and long shadows slip across the gravestones, you can feel your blood rising.

Risk Factor: 2

Apart from the difficulty of explaining yourself if you get caught—a zealous police officer might charge you with desecrating a grave—this location doesn't present many problems. Cemeteries are usually well kept and the grass is rather soft.

DO IT (NOW):

Gravestones themselves don't provide a lot of cover, and actually doing it on the grave itself presents a big ick factor. Fortunately, most cemeteries contain tombs—small free-standing buildings—which provide cover. Spread a blanket down behind one, out of sight, and wait for the early evening when a gentle breeze is blowing and the air smells like gladiolas. If you can get away with it, bring a bottle of wine to help the mood. Getting completely undressed isn't advised, since you may have to pull on clothes quickly if the night watchman hears anything.

Considerations:

Bats, mice, and open graves.

Chair Lift

That long ride up the mountain has you thinking about mounting your lover. If you can have a quickie in a chair, why not in a chair lift?

Risk Factor: 5

The caution "Remain seated at all times," unfortunately, precludes maneuvering yourself on top of your lover's lap for some lift-rockin' action. But fear not. Given a long enough lift, you might still bring it off.

DO IT (NOW):

Chair lifts are ideal for combining hand jobs with the mile-high club, so drape a jacket or blanket over your lover's lap, and see if you can beat your partner before the lift beats you to the top. By the time people on the other side of the lift, headed downward, realize what you're doing, they'll be long past and still scrambling to take a picture with their cell phone. If the chair lift is giving you a high-altitude tour of an amusement park, you're in more luck: not only will the trip be longer, but there are sure to be intermittent stops to allow more people to get on (or to get off, as the case may be).

Considerations:

Remember to bring tissues before you get on the lift, or departure will be a little sticky.

Chaise Lounge

A sunny day, the privacy of your backyard, a gentle breeze, and a chaise lounge for reclining: the perfect setting for a quickie that will shake the birds from the trees. Make lemonade.

Risk Factor: 1

Making love on a chaise lounge is far easier than doing it, say, on a three-legged stool or an ottoman. The length allows you to stretch out your legs or open 'em wide!

DO IT (NOW):

Not only is the chaise lounge optimal for a twosome, it's also perfect for the one-girl-two-guys threesome. So call over the pool boy and the guy mowing your lawn: it's time for a break. The first guy lies on the lounge as anyone normally would, except that he's naked and ready to pitch a tent. Ladies, lie on top with your back on his stomach and his manhood up your back door. This allows the second guy to mount missionary style. After a while, feel free to recline on the lounge, while the two boys stand on either side, fanning or providing shade. Your hands are occupied, working both fellas, as each guy offers a lemonade to suck through two straws!

Considerations:

Check the weight tolerance of the chaise before you do any of this.

Location 32:

Charity Dinner

Yeah, yeah, important cause, time to act is now, anything you can give, blah blah. All this talk about suffering and strife, combined with the fact that the second course is late, is making you hungry. All your hosts want is your money, so they won't mind if you skip out for a sec.

Risk Factor: 2

Charity dinners are a wonderful opportunity to engage in loutish, vulgar behavior because your hosts just want you to sign the big check. Show your support by being a regular at the cash bar, and get primed for a memorable night!

DO IT (NOW):

Every charity dinner has a long-winded appeal for money and someone "from the front lines" yammering on about their personal experience. That's the time you and your partner should quietly excuse yourself and find some room to have a knockdown pound-a-thon. Assure your hosts that you will be right back: you're just stepping out to call your accountant to check your liquidity. Charity dinners are often held in hotel ballrooms with handy access to stairwells, basement boiler rooms, broom closets, and other quickie locales.

Considerations:

If you get caught, remind your interloper that charity begins at home and you're feeling particularly generous tonight. Then sign the check.

Christmas Tree Farm

Ho, ho, ho, you ho! Time to deck the halls and jingle some balls! Put a live tree in your home this season, and the smell of pine will make you think you're doing it in the woods.

Risk Factor: 4

Picking a Christmas tree is a traditional family outing, which translates to the potential for little kids running in tears through the Douglas firs, asking Mommy why that man is hurting the nice lady.

DO IT (NOW):

Many Christmas farms allow you to "tag" your tree in the fall; that is, show up in early November, wrap a ribbon or tag around the tree you want, and come back in December. Go for this strategy to increase the odds for privacy. You don't want to go too early in the year, because you can't hide your quickie behind knee-high saplings. Go tagging early in the day on a weekday while the kids are still in school. Autumn temperatures also allow you to wear less clothing than if you went tree hunting in subzero temperatures.

Considerations:

If you happen to be caught doing it behind the trees, explain you wanted to get a jump on the season and have your yule log come early this year.

Location 34:

Church

If you're going to confession, it helps to have something to confess, right? And sometimes the spirit is willing and the flesh is just as willing! Balance out the spiritual with the physical. Just like Adam and Eve, be naked and be not ashamed.

Risk Factor: 5

If you're caught, you'll likely be tossed out of church, but beyond that, the Bible isn't terribly clear on what befalleth those who partaketh in a bang within the holy temple of God.

DO IT (NOW):

Some churches are open during the week, when services are not being performed, so this affords you the chance to sneak in under the pretext of silent prayer. If you go when confession is not being held, the confessional booth may be unlocked: go for it. Scope out the choir balcony; if you're discovered there, tell the janitor you're checking the organ. Resist the temptation to do it on the altar—that's just plain Satanic. Also avoid cries of "Oh God!" because churches have a terrific echo. If you're discovered, you might get away with saying you were having an ecstatic vision. And to anyone who asks what you're doing, just reply, "The missionary position!"

Considerations:

A $20 bill dropped in the poor box on the way out goes a long way toward reconciliation.

City Hall

It's a given that most of the politicians who inhabit city hall are self-serving, self-regarding, bureaucratic boobs. It's also a given that every chance they get, most of them are screwing their constituents. So why not return the favor by . . . well, you get the idea.

Risk Factor: 1

There are plenty of private places in city hall for you to do the deed without interruption. But even if you're caught, just do what any politician found with his pants down does: Call a press conference.

DO IT (NOW):

City halls come in all shapes and sizes, but they'll all have offices, closets, nooks, and crannies where you can engage in some quiet nookie. The best time is during meetings of city council, when everyone's attention is likely to be elsewhere. If city hall is particularly large, use one of the elevators. You'll have to be quick, between floors, but if necessary you can always push the emergency stop button and get a little extra time.

Considerations:

Patronage workers looking for a handout.

Location 36:

Classroom

This location ranks high on the list of porn flick scenarios, along with "Office," "Examining Room," and "Kitchen" (for when the plumber calls). We associate classrooms with hard lessons and strict teachers—or vice versa.

Risk Factor: 3

Obviously, you'll want to wait until class is dismissed, unless you've volunteered to demonstrate aspects of human biology. If you're discovered, people may object more your desecrating a place of innocence and education than to the fact that you've made a mess.

DO IT (NOW):

So you've found an empty classroom at your kid's open house or because you've broken into an abandoned school. Whatever scenario you play out (the student who really needs an A, the sex ed teacher), go for the teacher's desk instead of the student's desk: the latter can be wobbly and unstable. Make good use of props, such as the chalkboard or pillows used for Reading Circle. In teaching your partner the "three R's," don't neglect the "four O's," as in Oh! Oh! Oh! Oh!

Considerations:

Curious janitors are easily bought off, most of the time with permission to watch instead of with money.

Concert

You get to the rock concert on time, but come on, who listens to the opening act? Or to the slow ballad your favorite band recorded for that blockbuster movie? Instead of grabbing a beer, grab your partner.

Risk Factor: 3

Your risk depends on the music at the concert. If the headlining act is raucous and wild, this gives you permission to act like a savage lunatic. If you're at a classical music concert, you may also act like a savage lunatic, just not out in the open.

DO IT (NOW):

Choose a concert or concert venue that has low security, to decrease the likelihood of discovery. A stadium has plenty of stairwells and restrooms, and if you're in the money, you may have box seats, which allow you to have a quickie and order potato skins. No one's going to be looking in your direction anyway, so live it up. If you need a little foreplay, go buy a concert T-shirt and try on several sizes in front of your partner, settling finally on the extra small.

Considerations:

If you decide to give your lover oral sex right there in the stands, be prepared for cries of "Down in front!"

Confessional

If you're too shy to put into words what exactly you need to confess, you can always act it out for the priest's (and your) benefit. The priest is bound by a holy oath not to divulge what occurs in confession, so leverage this to your advantage.

Risk Factor: 3

Having sex in a confessional may leave you open to be struck by lightning, but it's also so weird and unnatural, it might turn out to be good luck. You never know until you try.

DO IT (NOW):

If you're not game on having someone listening in to you and your lover breaking a commandment, try entering the confessional booth when the sacrament is not being held. Get inside the church during a weekday, when next to no one is there. Now, the confessional door may be either an actual door or a heavy velvet curtain, which is meant to absorb sound (not *that* much sound!). Once inside, there may be only space to kneel, facing a corner. Your best bet, therefore, is rear-entry stand-up sex. The confessional may also be equipped with a box of facial tissue, which some people use for tears of regret. You'll find another use.

Considerations:

Once you've done the dirty deed, say a sincere prayer of apology to the Man Upstairs. He's the forgiving kind.

Location 39:

Convenience Store

Some people find the smell of Slurpies and stale donuts a turn-on. Others are intrigued by the idea of a very public venue for sexual experimentation. So give it some creative thinking, and turn that midnight run for a quart of milk into an erotic adventure.

Risk Factor: 3

While physically there isn't much in a convenience store that can hurt you (apart from the six-month-old Twinkies), chances of being found out are pretty high. And since convenience store clerks have the police department on speed dial, you may not have much chance to get away.

DO IT (NOW):

Most of the main part of the convenience store is out in the open, easily observable by the clerk and other patrons. Stores are also usually fitted with mounted mirrors to cut down on shoplifting. Your best bet is to sneak into the back area, around the ice machine and the shelves where overstock and cleaning supplies are kept. Choose a time when the clerk is busy with other customers; if you're the only ones in the store, you'll be conspicuous by your absence. Standing up while you do the deed is best. You *really* don't want to lie on that floor.

Considerations:

Late-night robbery attempts.

Corn Maze

You're dying to kiss your loved one behind the ears, so you head to a corn maze. Navigating a maze requires teamwork, patience, and cooperation, all the elements necessary for a good relationship and a five-star quickie.

Risk Factor: 4

The danger here is in getting turned around (and I don't mean on all fours).

DO IT (NOW):

Call ahead to your local farm and seek out the hardest corn maze within driving distance, because the harder the maze, the fewer the people and the more likelihood you won't get discovered. Your goal here won't be "solving" the maze, but diving sufficiently deep into it so that you can buy yourself some privacy. Your best bet here, given the narrow confines of the labyrinth, is down-and-dirty doggie style. First, find a dead end. Second, trace back about a hundred feet and lay a dry twig on the ground: this will be your alarm that someone's approaching. Then get busy, zip up, and find your way out.

Considerations:

If you're lost in the maze, you're surrounded by nutritious corn. Snack and survive.

Dance Floor

Everyone knows that you can tell how compatible two people are in bed by watching them dance. And depending on the groove, dance is humankind's most primitive and effective foreplay.

Risk Factor: 5

You know how everyone clears the floor when two really good dancers get going? The same will happen if anyone discovers you're having sex. Maybe you like to be watched or maybe it's too big of an audience, but the danger's the same.

DO IT (NOW):

Ladies, wear short skirts and no undies. Gentlemen, no undies and no short skirts—just pants. Hit the club where the number of dancers on the floor reaches the level of "fire hazard." Wait for them to release the soap bubbles or fog or hit the strobe lights. The ladies will have their purses and access to some handy lubrication, and once you've found a good corner, make your move and get in the groove. Public sex on the dance floor hasn't been in vogue since Studio 54 closed up shop, so you may get a few stares. Just tell any gawkers that you're doing a new version of "The Bump."

Considerations:

Someone may want to "cut in." Tell him your lover's dance card is full, thanks.

Location 42:

Deck

Whether you build it yourself or have it installed, you will want to test your deck for stability and strength. A rowdy quickie is better than a safety inspector any day of the week.

Risk Factor: 2

Unless your deck was built by illegals or your brother-in-law, it's not going to collapse under the weight of intercourse. Remember that you also need privacy. Keep the noise down and the profile low.

DO IT (NOW):

The deck, as a place to have sex, is like your bedroom with a railing to hold onto, so make good use of it. Depending on the quality of the deck material, you may also want to lay down an outdoor carpet first, to prevent getting splinters. Sitting on the railing in a sex position may have its charms, but hold onto something for leverage: you don't want to fall over backwards onto the grill or into the gardenias. If you need privacy, consider pitching a tent on your deck, and if the deck backs up to nothing but the woods, be as wild as you like. Try manning the grill with a "Kiss the Chef" apron and nothing else.

Considerations:

See the "Chaise Lounge" entry for more ideas, should your deck be large enough to accommodate it.

Desk

Whether you're a teacher, an executive, or an office worker, sometimes you just don't want to wait for a more convenient place. Under the gentle glow of a computer monitor—and a quick check to make sure the office door is closed— clear some space for a desktop dalliance.

Risk Factor: 1

Especially in a closed office, particularly one with a lock on the door, you're not in danger of interruption. The biggest concerns are not to break anything—like your computer!—by bumping into it and dealing with the smirks from your fellow workers as you walk out of the office.

DO IT (NOW):

Clear some space quickly. If you're not too concerned with noise and if there's nothing obviously breakable on the desk, make a dramatic gesture and sweep everything onto the floor. A loud crash can be a turn on. Of course, you may have to push the computer monitor to one side and make sure there aren't any loose pencils, pens, or paperclips lying about. After that you can get down to serious business. The man lies on the desk, while the woman straddles him. Since you've got some privacy, enjoy it and get naked. Oh, and be sure to tell your admin to hold your calls.

Considerations:

Cell phones and inconvenient window washers.

DMV

Nothing says "fun" like going to a place where the lines are longer than the ones in Disneyland, except that there are no rides. And no cotton candy. Put it in overdrive! Spice up the DMV!

Risk Factor: 5

While most people at the DMV wouldn't blame you for introducing some fun into an afternoon wasted, the DMV usually has security or police around.

DO IT (NOW):

Taking a date to the DMV allows you to wait in line while your partner cases the joint for available hideaway spots. If nothing is available, or you must go alone, ask the person taking your driver's license photo if she enjoys "candid photography" or "adult glamour shots." You may win a private session in the employee locker room. If you're filling out your one-hundredth form, ask the bored hottie behind the desk if, under "Sex," you may write, "Anytime, anywhere." This subtle hint will tip her off as to your ulterior motives. Your orgasms are sure to be in triplicate.

Considerations:

Beware of DMV VD.

Dock

Who doesn't like seamen? Traditionally, boats in port are christened with a shattered bottle of champagne—not very eco-friendly! Instead, sacrifice a maidenhead for that maiden voyage.

Risk Factor: 3

The cover of night will afford you more privacy, and seafarers, being superstitious, may allow public fornication as a way of inviting good luck. Sailors also understand getting some before you leave port.

DO IT (NOW):

Avoid the docks of your local yacht club, because expensive boats are monitored by expensive security: cameras, alarms, men in ascots. Obscure your activities with some carefully placed lobster traps. If discovered, explain that ordinarily you would screw on your boat, but the motion makes you seasick: docks are far sturdier. If you really want to play with people's minds, dress up in ghostly attire and announce to any interlopers that you are wandering spirits from the doomed ship *The Humping Dutchman*, and that ye who meddle with the captain's log shall suffer the torments of a watery grave. Punctuate with "Arr!"

Considerations:

Make sure doing it by the shrimp boats doesn't send you home with the crabs.

Doctor's Office

You're going for an annual checkup. You ask your significant other to come because you're afraid of shots. Instead of reading a magazine while you wait, you start playing doctor.

Risk Factor: 2

You definitely don't want to get caught. Even though you have a whole room to yourself while you wait, you don't want your doctor to walk in on you getting busy. They're supposed to do the exam, remember?

DO IT (NOW):

Waiting for a doctor can take a good 20–30 minutes. So speed won't be a factor here. Having someone come into the room with you is not that unusual, especially if you explain to the nurse that going to the doctor makes you anxious. If you are going in for a checkup or exam, your nurse will ask you to undress and put on a gown. If you have to be naked anyways, why not have some fun while you wait? The gown is usually made of paper and therefore very delicate. Don't bother putting it on until you are done. Your best bet is to use the exam table to your advantage. Ladies, the stirrups at the end of the table may come in particularly handy.

Considerations:

Tell your doc you thought your partner was her new assistant!

Drive-In

Drive-in movie theaters introduced the Baby Boomer generation to making out in cars (as well as to monster movies no one watched). Indulge in American nostalgia and pretend you and your partner are the high school football captain and head cheerleader out on a big date.

Risk Factor: 3

Doing it at a drive-in is only slightly less risky than doing it at the movies. Your rocking car will give you away, and leaves you vulnerable to jackass teens who'll deflate your tires or throw fries at your windshield.

DO IT (NOW):

Your safest bet here is to go to a drive-in that's been abandoned for years. Chances are there's one in your vicinity. Don't park in the middle of the empty lot, as this will look conspicuous (that and the fact that there's no movie showing). Rather, isolate yourself in a corner and lock your doors in case there are any drug dealers sharing your space. If you are truly in an abandoned territory, feel free to get busy on the hood of your car!

Considerations:

Make it quick and get out of there, 'cause one time I saw this movie. These teens were makin' out at an abandoned drive-in and this kid who'd been murdered there years before rose from the dead and . . . hey! Where ya goin'? Aren't you stayin' for the second feature?

Drive-Thru

It seems these days that more and more services are drive-thru: food, liquor, banks. Since you spend so much time waiting in line for the person ahead of you to place his order, you might as well put that time to good use.

Risk Factor: 1

There's no physical problem involved (aside from the awkwardness of being in a car), and since you're mobile, you can make a quick getaway in the event you're discovered.

DO IT (NOW):

Since drive-thru lines keep moving, full-out sex probably isn't an option; there's too much risk of getting interrupted by an impatient horn sounded by the person behind you. It's best to do this late at night, when there's not going to be many people around. Given the need for speed and discretion, oral sex is the way to go. Think of it as an appetizer to the main course you're picking up at the window. The man should do the ordering, taking his time, while the woman loosens her seat belt and leans over him. Just remember to finish up by the time you're at the window. There's nothing worse than having an attendant ask if you'd prefer something be super-sized.

Considerations:

Unexpected two-way video screens at the ordering station.

Location 49:

Dump

Why have sex at the dump? Why *not* have sex at the dump, I say. The very fact that no one in their right mind would expect you to have sex at the dump makes it the perfect opportunity.

Risk Factor: 2

The danger here is for the wind to shift in your direction. Also, the ground can get a little slippery and uneven. Wear heavy boots, and little else.

DO IT (NOW):

Consider going at twilight or later, as this affords you some privacy, but be sure to bring strong flashlights so you won't step into something you can't identify by sight or smell. Find the ubiquitous "dump sofa," and isolate the cleanest spot. Some people get turned on by dirty talk; you may get turned on by the dirty smell. And the powerful aroma may distract your mind long enough to prolong orgasm. Like discoveries in the trash, the possibilities are endless. Best of all, you don't have to worry about not making a mess or breaking whatever you're having sex on. Go crazy! Just be sure to share a long, hot shower when you get home.

Considerations:

On your way back to your car, be on the lookout for discarded table settings. You wouldn't believe what some people throw out!

Elevator

Nothing brings out the tiger inside like a long elevator ride after a night on the town. All dolled up in your best rags and jewels, you're both high on the awesome time you had. As the elevator doors close, you can't take your hands off of each other.

Risk Factor: 2

There's no real danger in the elevator. Getting caught by the guard or doorman watching the cameras will probably mean exchanging sly smiles in the morning as you leave for work.

DO IT (NOW):

Unless you're in a swanky sky rise, there shouldn't be surveillance. Once inside the elevator, flip the emergency brake to extend your stay. Now you can get busy. The man should remain standing and hoist the woman up. She can wrap her legs around the man's waist. For a little more friction, the man can lean forward and rest her back on one of the elevator walls. Beware that the emergency brake signals the authorities so frolicking is limited. Once you're both spent, tidy up and wait to be rescued by the concerned local authorities.

Considerations:

Not being rescued for a very long time.

Factory

A factory's successful operation depends on manpower, long hours, and repetitive motion. Sound familiar? Fortunately, the union has negotiated a midafternoon break.

Risk Factor: 2

As long as the bottom line is not imperiled, you and your partner will likely get off with a warning. If management presses, argue sexual discrimination: You can't fire someone for having sex on the job.

DO IT (NOW):

Volunteer for the graveyard shift, and plan with your partner to take your break at the same time. The noise of machinery will likely mask your moans and even howls of pleasure. Another strategy is to show up early and leave a little early, and to time your climax with the end-of-shift whistle. An excellent candidate for your on-the-job quickie is the quality control manager, since he or she is a master of efficiency and time conservation. Hey, they're just doing their job! A third approach is to hold your quickie in an abandoned factory, but stay away from old ones: you don't want the floor to give out underneath you.

Considerations:

Safety first.

Family Reunion

I know what you're thinking: Have a quickie with someone in my family? Gross! Disgusting! Illegal in most states! Hang on, now. Hot sex is supposed to be transgressive.

Risk Factor: 1

Should you be caught, you probably won't be invited back to a family reunion ever again, which may be what you're shooting for in the first place!

DO IT (NOW):

Search out those cousins who are fourth- or fifth-removed, because you share as much blood with them as you do with the nearest telephone pole. If you only have first cousins in attendance, hit on their dates or spouses because rest assured, amigo, they'd rather be somewhere else doing something fun—hopefully, you. Ask if they, like you, possess the secret family birthmark, which you'd be happy to show them in private. Thirty seconds into your quickie, and they'll forget all about what you'd promised to show them. Staying close with your family is important, and you've never felt family ties until a member of your family has tied you up.

Considerations:

If all goes well, you may volunteer to be on the next reunion's organizing committee!

Location 53:

Farm

They don't call it a roll in the hay for nothing. In a big barn on a lazy Saturday afternoon, earthy smells all around you, and the gentle mooing of cows in thc distance—climb up to the hayloft, stretch out, and get country.

Risk Factor: 1

Assuming the farm in question belongs to you or your family, there's no real danger. If you've sneaked on to someone else's farm, things could go dramatically different, but even then you're probably all right if you keep out of sight and are quiet.

DO IT (NOW):

Hay or straw might look soft, but it can be pretty prickly if there's nothing between it and your bare skin. A blanket or soft clothing is advised. The hayloft or some other out-of-the-way place is best if you're not supposed to be there. Keep away from animal stalls, since loud noises are apt to excite them. In the middle of the afternoon, everyone's out in the fields, so there's less chance of interruption.

Considerations:

Farmers with pitchforks.

Fast Food Restaurant

On one of those nights when you don't feel like cooking or staying on your diet, you find yourself in the mood for a Really Happy Meal.

Risk Factor: **4**

Fast food restaurants pride themselves on cleanliness. If you can't bring a dog into the place, they're certainly not going to look favorably on you assuming the doggie position. Even if you wash your hands afterward.

DO IT (NOW):

Your best bet is to wait until after midnight, which is the time when fast food restaurants attract local weirdos, drug users, and deviants. The rest room is clean and may have a door that locks. Also, the parking spaces behind the restaurant will surely be abandoned. Just don't have your quickie behind the dumpster, because this is the time-honored traditional spot where people in the food service industry fuck. (Gross, I know, but so is the job.) Remember that anyone who works at a fast food restaurant is making minimum wage and never gets tips, so they are easily bought off.

Considerations:

Offer to buy the officer a combo meal—and supersize it.

Ferris Wheel

A guy wins his gal a Kewpie doll, and she thinks he's just swell. A shared corn dog, a trip through the Tunnel of Love, and now it's time for a little Ferris Fuck.

Risk Factor: 5

Amusement park rides are engineered to induce vomiting. Throwing sex into the mix is truly risky business. Plus, there are kids everywhere. Good timing and fancy fingerwork will help you here.

DO IT (NOW):

Tell the ride operator that your partner is horny for heights and there's a twenty-spot in it for him if he can make sure you're stuck at the top for a couple of minutes. Once there (and assuming you've revved each other up with plenty of foreplay), go for manual or oral stimulation. Remember you are strapped in, so missionary is out. For those afraid to fly, this is the equivalent of the mile-high club. Drape a jacket over your lover's lap, for added discretion. As they say at the carny games, "everyone's a winner." Do your best not to rock the seat too much: you'll attract either too much attention or waves of nausea.

Considerations:

Bring along a hand wipe. You don't want to give a hand job with fingers sticky from cotton candy.

Location 56:

Ferry

To quote from Edna St. Vincent Millay's poem "Recuerdo": "We were very tired, we were very merry — / We had gone back and forth all night on the ferry." I bet you did, Toots.

Risk Factor: 3

Yours truly has made out on a commuter ferry, with no one else aboard and the captain's back turned to us. Spray from the harbor was some interference, but if you're going to get wet . . .

DO IT (NOW):

If you cannot find a small ferry ensuring privacy, there are large ferries with plenty of room to hide (e.g., the ferry that can take you and your car to an offshore island vacation spot). Be sure to take motion sickness pills if a rockin' boat makes you queasy, and if you swing a make-out spot on the upper deck, be wary of the weather: it can get very cold on the open water without the sun, and a rain slicker may provide coverage for your dirty deeds.

Considerations:

The captain has the power to marry you, so unless you're already married, be sure he doesn't sneak up on you and declare you husband and wife.

Location 57:

Firehouse

Fire in the hole! Whip out the hose! It's time for five-alarm sex! And by "firehouse," we mean the headquarters of the fire department, not a house that happens to be on fire.

Risk Factor: 4

Everyone knows that firefighters are in most women's Top Five Fantasies, so if someone discovers you, they'll be surprised but not shocked. Sex in the firehouse has been done in the movie *Backdraft* and in *Sex and the City*.

DO IT (NOW):

Ladies, there's no big trick to dating a firefighter. If you showed up at the firehouse in your best fuck-me outfit and said you wanted to repay local heroes for all their hard work, you'd have to fight them off. But guys, buddying up to your local firefighters won't be enough to "borrow" their barracks: you'll need a major bribe, which is of course frowned on by the law. Your best bet is to join the volunteer fire department and gain access to the building. Once inside, there's no telling when you'll have enough time for your quickie, which is part of the thrill.

Considerations:

Firefighters wear suspenders to keep their pants up. Undo those, and you're golden.

Fireworks Display

In the movies, fireworks have almost always been used as a metaphor for sexual climax. If you time things right (and the timing is everything) you can make your own fireworks while everyone else around you is looking at the sky. On a hot July night, get ready to turn up the heat.

Risk Factor: 2

Really, if you're discreet, you'll be able to get away with a lot and no one around you will be the wiser. At worst, those sitting near you may be wondering where those noises are coming from.

DO IT (NOW):

The trick here is to bring a blanket that's not only big enough to lie on but large enough to wrap over yourselves. Choose a spot a bit away from the rest of the crowd but with an unobstructed view of the fireworks. When the display gets going, the woman lies on her side under the blanket while the man enters her from behind. Time your movements to the explosions overhead. If you manage things just right, you may both finish just as the final massive barrage is exploding in the sky over you. That's a sight and sensation neither of you will forget.

Considerations:

Stray firecrackers and skyrockets.

Fitting Room

You and your hot new romance are walking the crowded corridors of a favorite department store. After shopping for hours in the midst of screaming toddlers, impatient parents, and trendy teens you head for the fitting room. While she tries on dress after dress, you both decide you're hungry . . . not for food, but for each other.

Risk Factor: 2

There's no real danger in having a bit of fun in the fitting rooms (except for the occasional rug burn or pin prick). But if caught you can be banned from the store or harassed in the backroom by an obviously jealous store manager.

DO IT (NOW):

Though fitting rooms themselves lack surveillance, many stores have them on the sales floor. To avoid detection, casually check for cameras on the way into the fitting rooms if they're not unisex. If there are cameras that move, wait until they're turned in another direction before you enter. For still cameras, walk close to the wall and enter the fitting room. The privacy of the fitting room allows you to have fun in lots of ways. One good way is for the woman to get on her knees on the bench so graciously provided by management while the man remains standing. This way passersby see one set of legs and it's assumed all is well.

Considerations:

Commissioned salespeople.

Location 60:

Funeral

It might, at first, seem disrespectful, but when you think about it, what better way to celebrate someone's life than bringing a little more happiness into your own lives? While others are talking about how much the Departed loved life, create a little tribute of your own.

Risk Factor: 3

The consequences of being exposed (so to speak) will probably be pretty devastating. Discovery could possibly cause a serious breach with your or your partner's family and friends, so extra caution is called for.

DO IT (NOW):

Find a back room in the funeral home, church, synagogue, or wherever the service will be held. You might need to scout this out beforehand. Ideally, the room should have a lock on the door and be one in which you're unlikely to be disturbed. To avoid being detected, either do the deed during the viewing or, possibly, immediately after the conclusion of the service when everyone is milling around. Speed is essential; if you're gone too long, it will excite comment and some busybody is likely to come looking for the two of you. In keeping with the spirit of the event, black lingerie and stockings are recommended.

Considerations:

Clergymen looking for a restroom.

Garage

Having a close, trusting relationship with your auto mechanic cannot be underestimated. If your local garage has a strict policy against accepting monctary tips, you may have to offer something else.

Risk Factor: 2

Motorheads and grease monkeys know how to keep secrets (like the fact that they screw with your car so you'll be back in another month or so). Plus, zipping them out of those work suits is quick and easy.

DO IT (NOW):

Plan your rendezvous for after hours at the garage. To get both your engines running, bring plenty of lubrication. Once the stick shift has been tested, it's time to get it in gear. You may get some additional privacy by doing it in a car that's on a lift, but this may require a third party to get you up there and get you down. Bring along a rag to wipe up any spilled fluids or to clean the dipstick. With a few twists and hard turns, that baby will be running smooth and purring like a kitten. Plan your next checkup for, say, the following weekend. You can't be too careful. Or horny.

Considerations:

Grease-black hand prints on your ass.

Location 62:

Gas Station

Given the cost of filling up your car these days, you might as well get something extra when you stop at a gas station. Cars in and of themselves are sexy, and on a summer evening the odor of gasoline can be intoxicating. So get ready to fill more than just your gas tank.

Risk Factor: 2

There's not much danger if you take a few precautions. Privacy, as always, is the main issue, and there are several ways to stay out of sight. As long as you're not trying for something in the middle of the gas pump island, you're probably fine.

DO IT (NOW):

Ask the attendant if you can use the restroom. When he gives you the key, walk casually around the side of the station, keeping an eye out for other cars. Your partner can slip quietly out of the car when the attendant's back is turned and join you in the bathroom, where you can have some privacy. Since a lot of gas station bathrooms aren't . . . *hrm!* . . . as sanitary as they might be, standing up and remaining mostly clothed is a good idea. Don't take more than five minutes, or the attendant's liable to get curious.

Considerations:

Minivans filled with small children, all needing to use the bathroom.

Gazebo

Having a quickie in a gazebo is like doing it in your own little outdoor Greek temple. It's pastoral, passionate, and if it starts to rain, you have a roof overhead.

Risk Factor: 2

Your only risk here is if you do it in a gazebo not located in the privacy of a backyard (e.g., in a park on the Fourth of July or on the floor of a gazebo showroom). Remember there are no walls to absorb sound, and no front door to lock.

DO IT (NOW):

Take some time to set the scene: head out to the gazebo with some lemonade or mint juleps, some relaxing chairs, and a few citronella candles to keep the bugs away. Note to your partner that the word "gazebo" derives from the Latin word for "I will see"; then ask if your lover would mind showing you a little something. Make good use of the hand railings and roof supports: this is a sturdy structure that can take a little shaking. The nice part about the gazebo is that you can hold your quickie there in spring, summer or fall, and possibly even winter.

Considerations:

Remember that if you can see out, other people can see in.

Golf Course

Did you know that two famous movie stars conceived their child on the bridge between the seventeenth and eighteenth holes at St. Andrews's Old Course? It's true. And there's no place like a golf course for soft, well-tended grass and sandy bunkers. Stretch out and go for a hole in one.

Risk Factor: 3

Aside from the public nature of golf courses and the fact that you'll be banned for life if you're caught— not to mention public indecency charges—there's the danger of flying golf balls if you do it during playing hours.

DO IT (NOW):

If you can manage to get into the course after dark, things are fairly simple. Find a secluded spot, possibly a bunker on the sixth or seventh hole away from visible buildings. You won't need a blanket; the grass and sand will give you just what you want. If you choose to try it when people are actually playing, things become trickier. If the course contains any wooded areas, these are likely to provide the greatest amount of privacy, though you'll still have to watch out for golfers slicing into the rough. For extra credit, try out one of the water hazards.

Considerations:

Ground hogs.

Location 65:

Graduation

The best days of your life are about to come to an end, and you may never see some of your classmates ever again. Um, hello? Is there a more celebratory and appropriate occasion for quickies? Forget signing someone's yearbook: give them something they'll really remember you by.

Risk Factor: 1

Let me repeat: You probably won't see these people ever again. And you are wearing an outfit that may as well be a toga. And if it's 10:30 in the morning, you're probably already drunk. This is all very low-risk.

DO IT (NOW):

Given how hot it is that day, you weren't planning on wearing a stitch under that graduation robe anyway. So gents, strap on some sandals, and ladies, reach for your high heels. Classroom buildings are all vacant, as are your dorms, so you have more than enough potential places to grab a savory quickie. Even if you get caught, don't sweat it: Every adult there is thinking fondly of their past and wishing they were young again. Instead of getting a reprimand, you're more likely to receive a thumb's up and "Enjoy it while you can, kids."

Considerations:

Make this a special time, when you graduate "cum loudly."

Location 66:

Grocery Store

Food porn, supermarket as meat market, cleanups in aisle five—the grocery store practically insists at every turn that couples start copulating amidst the fresh scents and rock-bottom deals. The produce section alone is an erotic playground that would make Caligula faint.

Risk Factor: 4

You're lucky if you can find the rest rooms in a grocery store, never mind someplace you can go down on your lover with a little privacy, if you don't mind.

DO IT (NOW):

The easiest access to the employee sections of the grocery store is often the swinging doors in the butcher or seafood sections. Once you're through, the key here is to walk with confidence and purpose. If anyone asks who you are, the words "safety inspector" or "health department" will strike enough fear in their hearts for them to back off quick. Case the joint quickly. Look for employee locker rooms, dry goods storage, rest rooms, or a mammoth stack of cereal boxes to hide behind. Once there, use to your best advantage that zucchini or banana you swiped from the produce section.

Considerations:

If you are discovered, say that you heard there was a sale on pork this week.

Gun Range

C'mon, people. Guns were invented because the caveman's club was too heavy and cumbersome as a phallic symbol. Guys go nuts for chicks packing heat, and ladies like the control over something powerful going off in their hand.

Risk Factor: 5

The danger comes from the gun, not from the range. Be sure, when you have your quickie, that all firearms have been opened and checked for live ammo. Don't guess: look. Now you're sure. And never, ever point a gun at something you wouldn't want to shoot.

DO IT (NOW):

Safety first, followed quickly by protection. Your time on the range will get your adrenaline flowing and your heart rate excited. Once you're primed and ready for a different discharge, put the guns aside and scope out a make-out spot: the locker rooms, the rest rooms, or, if the range is outdoors, somewhere in the bushes that is clear out of range area. Focus on your target, apply pressure to your lover's trigger, and fire at will. Ladies, encourage your lover to hit your bull's-eye; gentlemen, you may fire when ready.

Considerations:

At least one of you may be shooting blanks.

Gym

Let's get physical! Everyone knows that exercise is easier with a partner to urge you on and make everything fun. Wait, are we still talking about working out in a gym?

Risk Factor: 5

Despite being surrounded by half-naked sweaty people, gyms have been known to ban people for far less than public fornication (e.g., not wiping down equipment afterward).

DO IT (NOW):

Your best bet here is to set up a gym in your own living space. Even if you live in an apartment, you can clear the floor and designate it a gym *pro tempore*. Seeing your gym as a potential fucking space may inspire you and your partner to get off the sofa (and not use the sofa for getting off). Yoga has plenty of exercises for couples, and someone doing sit-ups always needs someone to hold their knees (together or apart). Once you've worked up a healthy sweat, hit the showers together. Even if you don't lose weight, the fact that you're trying and working out with your partner will be a major turn-on.

Considerations:

Consume an energy bar during your workout for added endurance.

Location 69:

Halloween Party

Any occasion to dress up is an opportunity to dress down, and this popular holiday practically insists on wild and extroverted behavior. What's more, you and your partner are being someone (or something) else for a night, so racy behavior can be excused as all part of the holiday fun.

Risk Factor: 0

Ladies, this is the only night of the year when you can dress and act as slutty as you want, and everyone will tell you, "You look terrific!" If you get caught tonight, the general reaction will be, "What did you expect?"

DO IT (NOW):

Chances are, the Halloween party is in a friend's house, which means you can steal away to the master bedroom or den, lock the door, and get busy. Best of all, you can incorporate into your costumes whatever toys or accessories you use in the privacy of your bedroom! Hell, you could both dress up in your leather outfits, complete with masks and high-heeled boots, and call it a "costume." (No need to tell people that this is how you dress every Thursday night!) Be sure to partake of the spiked punch, too—alcohol intake can further support your excuses and heighten fantasies.

Considerations:

Too much candy is fattening. Sex has no calories.

Location 70:

Hammock

The backyard on a lazy summer afternoon. A couple of glasses of wine, a soft breeze ruffling the leaves overhead, and a big, comfortable hammock swinging between two trees. What could be a better place and time to engage in a little outdoor swinging sex?

Risk Factor: 2

Privacy isn't an issue, but balance certainly is. Hammocks are sturdy but they can tip easily, especially smaller ones. Falling on the ground isn't likely to heighten the romantic mood.

DO IT (NOW):

Up-and-down motion is fine; side-to-side movements aren't recommended. The missionary position works best with the least chance of spillage (of you, we mean). Getting undressed before you both get into the hammock is a good idea, since wriggling out of your clothes is likely to tip you over. A couple of small pillows make everything perfect.

Considerations:

Neighbor children with binoculars.

Hardware Store

Ladies, have you ever found yourself in need of a good tool for some nailing? Gents, is all your carpentry work tongue and groove? Your local hardware store has everything you need.

Risk Factor: 5

Hardware stores are all business. Everything and everyone there is all about work, work, work. While there's lots of sexual innuendo and double entendre, there's not much tolerance for slacking off on the job.

DO IT (NOW):

The least populated part of any major hardware store is the plumbing section: this is because your average customer leaves this work to the experts. Bear in mind, too, that the weekends (especially holiday weekends) are the busiest times for hardware stores. Your best bet is to hit the hardware store during a weekday. If it's raining or snowing, try the lumber section— no one's going to be shopping for outdoor supplies. In winter, go to the abandoned garden section. You'll have to put a little thought into this one! Remember to get the right tool for the right job.

Considerations:

If you're discovered, apologize and say that you were just looking for a good screw.

Hay Ride

Ladies, all it takes is a coy look and a stalk of hay in your mouth for your man to fall waist deep into a fantasy of Midwestern farmers' daughters. Fellas, all ladies like an outdoorsy type. Time to hit the hay!

Risk Factor: 3

Um, naturally, you don't want to get busy on a hay ride with other people and their kids, unless you want to divert attention away from the fornicating bulls. On the plus side, the tractor pulling you on the hay ride will drown out any noise you make.

DO IT (NOW):

Secure a hay ride for just you and your partner, and make sure it's a long one (the ride, silly goose). For insurance, you might stack a bale or two at the back of the hay bed, near the driver, so if he turns around, he won't see a thing. Don't wear farmer's overalls, as these don't provide the easiest access for lovemaking. Ladies, go for a skirt and cowboy boots, and gents, stick with jeans. Don't worry about rocking the bed, as field paths tend to be bumpy anyway.

Considerations:

Be sure you're not allergic to hay. You don't want to find out the hard way.

Location 73:

High School Reunion

Remember the really hot girl you lusted after during your junior year? Or the totally dreamy guy from the basketball squad you could never bring yourself to talk to? Now five, ten, or even twenty years later, here's your chance. High school reunions seem to make time stand still and send us back to the age of sixteen when the world seemed like a simpler place. You just need a little privacy and you're good to go.

Risk Factor: 1

Unless one or both of you are married to other people and your spouses are around, there's really no danger. Covert sex is an expected part of high school reunions, and it probably won't even raise any eyebrows if you're caught—though the online gossip mill at Classmates. com may get busy for a while.

DO IT (NOW):

If the reunion is held in your old high school, the possibilities are endless. The coolest thing is to sneak off to one of your old classrooms—maybe the one where the History teacher, old Mr. Kerflunkowitz, droned on endlessly about the Peloponnesian War. Draw the shade over the window, and lock the door. If there's no lock, a chair jammed under the doorknob will work. Then put Mr. Kerflunkowitz's desk to work. For extra daring points, leave a note on the chalkboard (D.A. and R.F. did it!).

Considerations:

Other couples with exactly the same idea.

Location 74:

Hiking

When you're out on a hike, stopping to catch your breath and drink some water, why not take the opportunity to make the great outdoors the *really* great outdoors?

Risk Factor: **3**

Depending on where you hike, you may encounter other hikers. And depending on where you indulge in your quickie, naked flesh may get exposed to Nature's less attractive elements (e.g., mosquitoes, poison ivy, thorns). And then there's the buzzkill of getting lost. Any trip into the outdoors, for sex or otherwise, requires a healthy respect for Mother Nature.

DO IT (NOW):

Avoid the most popular hikes in your area. You'll want to find a hike with a suitable level of difficulty and privacy. Look for mountains that require an all-day climb (you're almost guaranteed no families there) or rock formations of variegated shape (good hiding places). The best scenario for sex while hiking is the overnight camp-out, which assures the privacy of a tent, a shared sleeping bag, and—if no one's around for miles—the freedom to hoot and holler.

Considerations:

Be sure to apply bug spray in advance, and pack an extra energy bar to regain stamina!

Horseback

Off for a quiet ride in the country? Why not spice it up a bit? A bit of fun atop a stallion or a mare can add a whole new meaning to the phrase "a long, hot ride."

Risk Factor: 4

You're on top of a live, temperamental animal, doing something unusual. The horse's reaction can be unpredictable, and, if you're not careful, dangerous. Falling off in the middle of things is bad enough, but the last thing you want to do is chase after a horse that's been spooked by strange things happening on its back.

DO IT (NOW):

The best situation is if both of you are riding only one horse. If that's not possible, stop and tether the other horse securely. The woman sits facing the man, her legs around him, arms around his neck for balance. The man puts his arms around the woman's waist and holds the pommel of the saddle. If the horse is actually moving at the time, its rhythm can provide a pleasant counterpoint to yours. If it's standing still, don't be violent in your movements, or you can startle it with possibly disastrous results.

Considerations:

Low-hanging branches over the trail.

Horse-Drawn Carriage

You and your significant other have a wonderfully romantic dinner at The Tavern on the Green and are taking the horse-drawn carriage back to your hotel. The night air is cool, the stars are out, and you're both a little tipsy. Time to *really* go for a ride.

Risk Factor: 3

This situation could rock the carriage enough to tip over.

DO IT (NOW):

Here's the best way to get away with this deed without the handler knowing what's going on. Begin the trip back sitting on your significant other's lap. A dress or a skirt is best worn for this occasion. Since a carriage ride is rather bumpy it makes this a very salacious rendezvous.

Considerations:

Horses fail to take into consideration the romantic nature of your situation prior to relieving themselves in the street.

Location 77:

Hospital

You're in a hospital bed, which is an inherently unpleasant place to be. The TV has three stations to choose from; there are no video games or computers, which makes for a pretty long and boring day. Your significant other is coming to visit, so you could really use a distraction.

Risk Factor: 1

Unless you are very wealthy you are not in a private room. In fact, privacy is the least of anyone's concern in a typical hospital environment. The only risk associated with getting caught is embarrassment. It is unlikely that you'll be punished. What are they going to do, withhold your Jello?

DO IT (NOW):

Your best chance of any privacy is the curtain. Anyone who's ever been to a hospital knows this is less private than the walls in a cheap hotel. So, if you're lucky, your roommate will be cool with dealing with the sex sounds coming from behind the curtain. But then there's the hospital staff. These people think it's okay to drop in and pull back the curtain at any given time for any given reason. So timing is everything. Your best chance of not getting caught is to do it at night. Tell the nurse your visitor is your spouse, and she'll let him stay after visiting hours.

Considerations:

Watch for the patient's IV line and be careful not to trigger any heart monitors or alarms!

Hot Air Balloon

So you'd love to join the fabled mile-high club, but you're afraid of setting foot on an airplane? No problem!

Risk Factor: 3

Hot air balloons, by design, were made for stand-up sex only; otherwise, the "basket" would be rectangular. Balloons don't have "auto pilot," either, so part of your brain will need to focus on something other than nookie.

DO IT (NOW):

Hire out a balloon and tip the pilot heavily: in cash, and later, in eye candy. Wait until you're safely over the treetops to start your aerial adventure, and, if possible, keep the rocking motion to a minimum. Gentlemen, if you're standing and your partner is on her knees, be sure to wave back to anyone on the ground. Ladies, watch your breathing, as the air can get a little thin that far up. In the event your pilot won't allow any hanky panky, ask to be dropped off momentarily in the nearest open field.

Considerations:

If, in the middle of sex, you notice that you are surrounded by fog, your pilot has become too distracted. You are in a cloud bank.

Hot Tub

Every man should know that a necessary precondition for getting a girl on her back, in the sack, is to relax her. And what relaxes more than a hot tub? Steamy, bubbly, melting flesh relaxation! Mmm . . . better hurry up with that quickie before she turns to jelly!

Risk Factor: 4

Staying in a hot tub for too long can make you lightheaded, so getting yourself all worked up won't help the sitch. Take care not to overdo it. Fortunately, we're in quickie territory here, so it should be speedy.

DO IT (NOW):

Naturally, you'll want a hot tub with privacy. That way, you can indulge without interruption and best of all, you can enjoy the hot tub naked. Oral sex is best in a hot tub situation. Warm water works magic on women, making her more game for going down on her guy than she otherwise might be on dry land. So take turns sitting on the edge of the hot tub, soaking your tootsies, while your partner goes to work. Give yourselves a break from hot immersion by getting off on a cool tile floor. Finally, bask in the afterglow with massaging jets warm water.

Considerations:

Fellas may not want to sit th "boys" in the soup for exte periods of time. Small do quick releases are best.

Location 80:

Igloo

Just because you're snowbound doesn't mean having a quickie outdoors is out of the question. In fact, your quickie in an igloo may be the hottest sex you've ever had!

Risk Factor: 1

A well-made igloo ensures privacy. No one knocks on an igloo door and there's no phone. Provided you create a buffer between the snow and your bare bum, there's no risk of frostbite or freezer burn.

DO IT (NOW):

Go to any department store and find an igloo kit, which is basically a plastic "snow brick" maker. Enlist your lover's help to ensure that your fun room is built to everyone's satisfaction (and fortunately, there's no arguing with your partner as to what color the walls should be). Once inside, you'll find that the confined space captures the shared body heat surprisingly well. Shed a few layers and go at it, and soon you'll feel like you're in a sauna. Make your quickie quick, however, so that you don't melt a wall and have the whole construction collapse on you. Busting out of the igloo and using its remains for a postcoital snow fight may be the most enjoyable part.

Considerations:

Neighborhood kids who ask to share the space with you.

Inner Tube

This instrument of summer fun is sure to inspire erotic thoughts, since it resembles a giant diaphragm. On a lake, an ocean, or just in your private pool, the inner tube unleashes your inner sex fiend.

Risk Factor: 2

This isn't like making love in a kayak: if you tip or roll over, it's easy to get out from under an inner tube. The most awkward thing is getting both of you on.

DO IT (NOW):

First, get an inner tube made for "tubing," or tube-skiing. These tubes are sturdy and strong. As for position, I'd recommend gentleman on bottom, lady on top. Take it slow, and remember that it's not the size of the tube, it's the motion of the ocean. Bear in mind, too, that for optimum privacy, you can always inflate the inner tube and put it on your bedroom floor. You'll get more bounce than your bed, but you may have some explaining to do to your roommates or kids who see you wheeling a massive inner tube into your bedroom. If you're out on a lake or the ocean, consider wearing life jackets. What? I didn't say you had to wear anything else!

Considerations:

Blow up the inner tube with a pump. Blow it up yourself, and you may be too winded for sex.

Jail Cell

The best jail cell sex is consensual. The other kind, not so much. And since they tend to segregate the sexes into separate cells, this quickie's a little tricky.

Risk Factor: 5

You would think the police wouldn't mind public fornication in jail cells, because if they arrest you, they don't have to transport you anywhere. All the same, the cops frown on cell shenanigans.

DO IT (NOW):

Your best bet here is to date a police or corrections officer: someone with access to an empty cell. You might also show up at your local prison, passing yourself off as the Mattress Inspector; then, once inside with a sexy guard, you learn why the slang term for guard is "screw." In any event, breaking into a jail cell for sex may be as difficult as breaking out of one. Once in, however, make good use of the bars for leverage. Your moans of pleasure may encourage your neighbors to request a conjugal visit with you, but be firm. You're there to ensure that someone pays his or her debt to society, in kind.

Considerations:

Depending on how good your partner is, he or she may "get off for good behavior."

Jetty

Landlocked lovers: A jetty is a structure like a pier or wharf that extends into a body of water. Speaking of extending into a body . . .

Risk Factor: 1
....

The jetty in the isolated lake or the wharf at midnight should give you adequate cover to get uncovered without being discovered. Just avoid the jetty that's manmade from large rocks, which can be dangerously slippery when wet.

DO IT (NOW):

Evaluate your potential jetty spot for safety, sturdiness, and sufficient room. Also note the water conditions, because if you're by the ocean, the last thing you want is a large wave dampening your spirits and sweeping you out to sea. Once you've secured your spot, hold your quickie at the very end of the jetty: the walk out there will build anticipation. Be quick, because depending on your jetty's location, it may serve as a docking point for sea craft large and small. If you're discovered, just say you were out to "get jetty wid it."

Considerations:

Be sure your quickie is a mutually satisfying experience, or else the long walk out to the end of the jetty will become the Walk of Shame back home.

Kitchen

You and your partner are throwing your first dinner party. You've been slaving all day over a feast of beef Wellington, pumpkin risotto, and fresh strawberries with crème patisserie, and things are starting to get hot in the kitchen. Unfortunately, your guests will arrive in ten minutes.

Risk Factor: 1

Your dinner party could be remembered for all the wrong reasons: burnt beef, scorched rice, the image of your naughty bits in the creamed corn.

DO IT (NOW):

The trick here is to do the deed while keeping things cooking. While the meat is resting, clean off some counter space by loading and starting the dishes. Prop the woman on the counter above the dishwasher, which will provide a boost of heat and vibration, as time is of the essence. If she wraps her legs around her standing partner for balance, her hands are free to whisk the crème.

Considerations:

Make sure your shirt is on right-side out. Always check for hair in the food before serving.

Location 85:

Ladder

Lovers of unequal height need a little boost to see eye to eye. Help your lover get a leg up by helping yourself up his or her leg. Ask your neighbor if you can make good on that offer to borrow anything, anytime.

Risk Factor: 5

If you look closely at the warning label on the ladder, you'll see that none of the graphics include coitus as an acceptable use of the ladder. The ladder may be on secure ground, but it doesn't mean you and your lover are.

DO IT (NOW):

Take one step at a time. Strip and use the ladder as an aid to oral sex. No more craning your neck! No more awkward bending over or being on your knees! Gentlemen, ascend the first two steps of the ladder and allow your tool to poke through the rungs; Ladies, stand on the ladder's opposite side, holding it steady, and do what comes naturally. Next, try intercourse but keep it to the lower steps. If you climb too high and rock too hard, you will have a difficult time explaining yourselves to the insurance agency.

Considerations:

Once you've "cleaned the gutters," you can use the ladder to . . . well, clean the gutters. I mean, have you been up there recently?

Location 86:

Large Boat

With the gently rocking waves, a boat's almost as good as a waterbed for enjoying and experimenting with one another. Of course, the size makes a difference; your technique in a speedboat will be distinct from the one you use in a thirty-foot yacht. But the cool sea breeze, the cries of the sea gulls, and the smell of salt air all make for a special experience.

Risk Factor: 1

This varies with the size and configuration of the boat, but short of running aground, there isn't much to worry about. Even if someone sees you, you're on your own property, so there isn't much they can do about it.

DO IT (NOW):

Assuming you're in a powerboat (say, ten feet long), use the cushions running along the sides for bedding. You can drag them onto the deck, if you prefer a bit more wiggle room. The boat shouldn't be running—unless someone else is steering it—but if the weather's calm, the waves will provide a rhythm against which you can time your movements for greater pleasure. Swimsuits are optional.

Considerations:

Roving Coast Guard cutters.

Laundromat

The gentle hum of the dryers, the rhythmic splashing of the washers. The warmth and the smell of liquid soap in the air. Laundromats provide a calm, soothing atmosphere that's great for sex. While your clothes are getting clean, you can get dirty.

Risk Factor: 2

Laundromats are pretty clean, so there's not much chance of physical injury. On the other hand, if you're caught, you might have to leave without your clothes (literally).

DO IT (NOW):

Choose a spot toward the back of the laundromat, as far as possible from the front door. For maximum privacy, either very late at night or midafternoon on a weekday work best. Floors in most laundromats are made of linoleum—hard, slippery, and uncomfortable. Instead, try standing up, one of you with your back to an operating dryer. The warmth from the dryer will relax you, and the noise will cover your gasps and moans. Totally naked is probably not the best idea; the risk of interruption is too great. Though you can always explain you're just doing all your laundry at once.

Considerations:

Accidentally inhaling bleach.

Location 88:

Laundry Room

The privacy of your own laundry room allows you to do many things you couldn't get away with in a laundromat: do your wash naked, smell your partner's underwear, and fold clothes wearing a bra as a hat.

Risk Factor: 0

The biggest danger here is not actually getting your laundry done. If your washer and dryer are in your basement, you're free to make as much noise as you like, and you can hear interlopers coming down the stairs.

DO IT (NOW):

Ladies, the one sure way to get your partner to have sex in the laundry room is to show up with a basket of dirty clothes and to be wearing nothing but your underwear. Tell him if that if he does the laundry with you, he'll get a lesson in separating delicates from towels, and darks from whites. Oh, and he might get a lesson in something else, too, if he's a good boy. Once the sorting lesson is over, tell him to take off your clothes and his, and sort them appropriately. Away you go!

Considerations:

Show him how tongues can be put on spin cycle.

Location 89:

Library

It's a Wednesday night. You've been stuck doing research in the library with your partner since midmorning. The prospect of combing through one morc periodical database makes your eyes ache. Instead, you and your literary lover decide to peruse the stacks for something a bit more . . . stimulating.

Risk Factor: 2

If caught, you'll definitely lose your library card. And steer clear of the rare-book shelves; besmirched volumes carry a hefty replacement fee.

DO IT (NOW):

Don't even think about those nice little "research rooms" with the convenient door and no windows. They're way too obvious—you're a sitting duck for patrolling librarians—and not nearly enough of a challenge. Instead, consult ol' Dewey for the stacks least likely to be patronized (in other words, skip "current fiction bestsellers" in favor of "classical Greek engineering"). Once you've found an obscure row, enlist the help of a rolling book-return cart for extra stealth. The task at hand is least conspicuous if the woman is bent to search the lower shelves, while the man assumes the position behind her. (Skirts and shorts are recommended for easier access. A longer jacket for the fellow adds privacy.)

Considerations:

Extreme quiet. Keep moaning and giggling to a minimum.

Lighthouse

Phallic symbols of the oceanside, lighthouses stand proud and erect, safeguarding seafarers by night and providing inspiration to lovers by day. When doing it on an open beach is out of the question . . .

Risk Factor: 1

Make some calls: you may find that lighthouses in your area are available as places to stay for a night or two. This ensures you terrific privacy, because you may be surrounded by water. If anyone draws near from any direction, you can hear them splash.

DO IT (NOW):

If you're renting a lighthouse, you may have caretaking responsibilities, so be a good guest and see that the light is turned on at night. Once you're done with the to-do checklist, it's time to do your partner. If you dare to hold your quickie near the lighthouse beacon, be warned: you and your partner may project a shadow of the two-backed beast onto the nearest frigate. Even if you get busy at the base of the lighthouse, you're still in the center of a giant dildo with crashing waves as background music.

Considerations:

Lighthouses typically aren't located in the center of town, so do any birth control shopping beforehand.

Location 91:

Limo

Let's face it: Limousines are just big sex machines. The combination of power, money, and roomy backseats is irresistible. No matter if you're on your way to a movie premiere, a company black-tie dinner, or a high school reunion, there's always time and space for a little fun and excitement.

Risk Factor: 1

The only real awkwardness is that someone else is driving the car. However, most limos have curtains that shield that backseat from the driver's seat, as well as a glass window that blocks out most sounds.

DO IT (NOW):

Don't undress all the way unless the ride is a really long one. But the seats should offer plenty of room to stretch out and enjoy yourselves. In-city trips present a few challenges, since sudden stops for traffic lights, stalled buses, and so on can jolt you onto the floor. But if none of that happens, you're golden. Just be sure to time things so that the chauffeur doesn't open the door to let you out when you're still . . . um . . . you know.

Considerations:

Nosey policemen giving out traffic tickets.

Lobby

Whether they're in a hotel, an airport, or a movie theater, lobbies offer lots of dark corners for doing dark deeds. Of course, they also offer a lot of people milling about with little to do but watch one another and read old magazines, so the name of the game here is discretion.

Risk Factor: 2

The only real danger is that of being caught and tossed out. A bit humiliating, to be sure, but involving no real physical peril. Still, the very public nature of lobbies does present a lot of problems for those who don't want their sex to be a spectator sport.

DO IT (NOW):

Lobbies often have nooks and crannies. In the case of hotels (and sometimes airports), they occasionally offer additional cover in the form of statues, fountains, or large potted plants. Standing up is advised; lying on the floor multiplies the possibility of discovery. If you're in an airport, try to time things with the boarding of a busy flight. Everyone will be so busy trying to get on the plane that they're likely to ignore suspicious noises coming from behind the pillar in the corner.

Considerations:

Fussy concierges.

Locker Room

The locker room is the only place where strangers can get naked in front of one another without concern for getting arrested. And since they're adjacent to gyms and other athletic places, the locker room quickie is the perfect wind-down (or warm-up) for exercise.

Risk Factor: 5

Locker rooms are not known for being coed, and other people are there to work out, not get worked up.

DO IT (NOW):

The easy way out is to try to sneak your partner into the locker room of your own gender when the locker room is quiet or sparsely populated. A quickie in the rest room or shower stall, and there you are. Well, that may work, but you won't get points for originality. A more imaginative approach is to have your partner dress up as a member of your own sex and accompany you into the locker room without anyone giving a second glance. Granted, it may take more work to turn a Hirsute Harry into a Shaved Sheila, but the whole enterprise will turn both of you on. And if you're discovered? Women won't think twice about athletic lesbians getting in a lather, and men will run for their lives at the sight of a man having sex with a dude with boobies.

Considerations:

Wear flip-flops. Those shower floors can get pretty gnarly.

Location 94:

Mall

A full day of shopping works up your appetite, maybe for something other than free samples in the food court. Put down your bags and pull up that skirt! This is one freebie you can't refuse!

Risk Factor: 5

Mall cops don't take kindly to shenanigans. They'll jump at the chance to actually provide security instead of walking idle miles up and down the storefronts.

DO IT (NOW):

Your best bet is the old reliable changing room in a major department store. Depending on the time of day, they're as good as abandoned and no one will think twice about you inviting your lover into the room for an opinion on how that outfit looks on you (or off of you). Keep the noise down, as you may have noticed your room does not come with a ceiling or walls that touch the ground. And for Pete's sake, don't think you're being funny or rebellious by wiping yourself dry with the dress you don't plan on buying anyway. That's just icky.

Considerations:

Try hitting the mall by midmorning, before the teenagers arrive and while the old folks are napping in the massage chairs.

Motorcycle

Motorcycles call up irresistibly sexy images of tight leathers and the open road. Ever since Peter Fonda and Dennis Hopper set out to discover America in *Easy Rider*, motorcycles have been about the freedom to define your life. So here's a chance to make a very defining statement . . . and have some fun.

Risk Factor: 3

Well, clearly you're not going to do anything while the motorcycle's in motion. At least we hope not. But even at rest, a motorcycle is a big piece of equipment that can fall over if it's moved enough. Just be careful, and you'll be fine.

DO IT (NOW):

Inside your own garage is best, since there's the least chance of interruption—assuming you've sent the kids over to the neighbor's house for the afternoon. Harley Davidson cycles work best, since they're big and solid. Stay away from crotch rockets, which are more likely to tumble over. Make sure the cycle's kickstand is down and secure. Consider bracing the cycle against the wall as well. The woman lies on the seat, her head propped against the handlebars, her legs resting on the man's shoulders. For some added fun, wear leather jackets.

Considerations:

An unexpected visit from the Hell's Angels.

Mountain Climbing

Climbing a mountain is a terrific way to literally elevate yourself above the world of small concerns and petty problems. And those cute shorts and heavy boots on your lover are nothing to sneeze at, either.

Risk Factor: 2

Naturally, the mitigating factor here is what kind of mountain you're climbing. If you tackle a moderately challenging one, you're less likely to run into casual climbers, but you don't want one so exhausting to scale that you reach the peak . . . well, without any pique.

DO IT (NOW):

As you admire the scenery in your ascent, keep an eye peeled for brush cover or rock formations where you can quickly peel off clothing. If your mountain climb involves rock climbing, make good use of your ropes and straps. An adventure into Mother Nature's territory should involve caution and planning. If you can hold out long enough to have your quickie at the very top of the mountain, you're in the best position to feel the entire earth move underneath you, but beware: the higher up you are, the thinner the air may be.

Considerations:

The bear who went over the mountain to see what he could see. How about some privacy, buddy, huh?

Location 97:

Movie Set

You're ready for your close-up and finally to take that advice to "get a grip on yourself," so you call the grip over and tell him to get on you. Lights! Camera! Really Hot Action!

Risk Factor: 2

Having an entire crew watch you have sex will either induce stage fright or the most screaming orgasm you've ever had. And since men need some time between orgasms, you may need to put this one to bed in one take.

DO IT (NOW):

Advances in digital cameras have made it possible for anyone to make their own movie. In your case, don't just prop one on a tripod and hope for the best: enlist a few people, men and women if you like, to help you and your lover make the best home porno possible. Use multiple angles and invite suggestions from the crew, based on videos they've seen or what they think you'll be good at. Your friends may be so turned on, they'll request a cameo. Improvise. This may be some of your best work.

Considerations:

Don't let your friends unionize, or production will be held up like you won't believe.

Location 98:

Movie Theater

You show up for a matinee and suddenly feel the urge to act like a teenager again. The movie theater has always been one of the most popular places to fool around.

Risk Factor: 1

With plenty of seats and a very dark setting, the danger rating is low. If you play this right you can get away with a lot—maybe even a double feature!

DO IT (NOW):

Pick a not-so-popular movie and go see it in the middle of the day or when the theater first opens. If you're lucky, there won't be anyone there. If you have company, pick a spot in the back row or seats in the corner that will keep you well hidden. The loud noise or explosions of an action flick will surely muffle your sex sountrack. Many theaters have adjustable armrests that lift up so you and your honey can be closer. Put up all of the arm rests that are near you. With a little maneuvering, you can lay down on the seats. Avoid lying on the floor. They sweep them in between shows, but you never know what you might sit in.

Considerations:

If you've ever been to the movies you'll notice that every once in a while a group of kids sneak in after the movie starts. Keep an eye out.

Museum

Museums may be full of stuffed caribou, classical mosaics, or ancient Estonian drinking cups, but one thing they all have is plenty of dark corners. See if you can find some sex-themed artifacts—say, wall paintings preserved from Pompeii—and you may get some creative ideas.

Risk Factor: 2

There's not much in a museum that can cause physical danger. The big risk comes from getting caught by irate guards and banned for life. But a little elementary caution should take care of that problem.

DO IT (NOW):

Stay away from any special exhibits that are likely to attract crowds. Your best bet for privacy is in a section of the museum no one's much interested in—say, the exhibit of eighteenth-century paperweights donated by a wealthy English patron. The guards wander from room to room. Wait until the custodian leaves, and then grab the five minutes or so before he comes back. Standing positions are best; getting on the floor involves more maneuvering around than is going to be comfortable or time-conscious. Remember not to knock over any of the glass cases or things could get a bit sticky (and not in a good way).

Considerations:

School field trips with guides.

Night Club

Like the song says: "Do a little dance, make a little love, and get down tonight." A night on the town is all about getting dressed in something you're going to enjoy taking off.

Risk Factor: 5

Bouncers are there to enforce the desires of management, which are: Buy overpriced drinks, have your fun, then take it outside (fights, fucking, vomiting).

DO IT (NOW):

Bouncers can be bought, if the price is right, so if a high-risk quickie is worth it to you, pay the bouncer to look the other way (or watch you, whatever turns you on). The night club bathroom is fair territory for your quickie, but bear in mind this is also where people take the opportunity to snort cocaine and bitch about their dates—not exactly the most romantic setting. Try asking the bartender if there is a private room where you can make a very important phone call. If that doesn't work, see the entry for "Dance Floor."

Considerations:

Be sure to hit a night club that's in proximity to other night clubs, in the event you get booted on your booty call.

Nudist Colony

Surrounded by naked people, tired of shuffleboard, and looking for a cheap thrill, you and your lover want to toss some spice onto the banquet of bare flesh set out before you.

Risk Factor: 5

Nudist Colonies—or "clothing-optional resorts"—typically don't look favorably on people banging in open view. The philosophy is to relax while it so happens that you are naked. Believe it or not, some people embrace nudism so they *won't* be ogled and seen as sexual objects. When everyone's naked, everyone's wearing the same thing.

DO IT (NOW):

Open sex, or even snuck sex, will likely get you ejected. Many nudist colonies ask guests politely not to stare at other people or send come-on signals. So for safety's sake, take your quickie behind a closed door: preferably your lodging or, discreetly, a changing room. Nudist colonies are places of respect as much as tolerance. But any overtly sexual behavior will have people thinking you're a perv.

Considerations:

Apply sunscreen head to toe. For some, that means a lot of territory to cover. Ask your partner to give you a hand (or two).

Ocean

The ocean's ability to inspire poetry, reflection, and contemplation of the eternal is well documented. Its potential as an awesome quickie spot has yet to be written, so get to work!

Risk Factor: 3

See below. Depending on your physical relationship to the ocean, you will need to bear certain safeguards in mind (and body).

DO IT (NOW):

The ocean affords multiple opportunities for the quickie. The quickie beside the ocean is best done at twilight or after sunset, but be warned that the temperature on the beach tends to dip sharply without the sun around. The quickie in the ocean will give you plenty of below-the-waist privacy, but the cold water may not help the guys get inspired. The quickie on top of the ocean—in a seagoing vessel— has its charms, so long as the vessel in question is stable; that is, do not attempt in an inflatable raft. Best of all, perhaps, is the quickie by the ocean. Rent a cottage or hotel room overlooking the water, keep the window open, and let the salt air and rhythm of the waves get you in the mood.

Considerations:

The nude swim is the most refreshing postcoital exercise known to humankind.

Location 103:

Office

Why do so many porn videos take place in the office? Because once you're at work, you're supposed to check your libido (and your personality) at the door. How dull! Instead of bringing your work home, bring a little home into the office—say, your bedroom.

Risk Factor: 4

Another reason why pornos take place in the office! Being caught in the office could cost you your job. But hey, high stakes reap big rewards!

DO IT (NOW):

Your best bet to having sex at work Is to have your own office with a door that locks and has blinds. Plan the quickie for a time when the only person around is the janitor, emptying the wastepaper baskets. Also be sure your office doesn't have surveillance cameras: evidence can be a drag. Once you're in the clear, your desk is the obvious choice for a bed substitute, but don't rule out the chair! Make this one enjoyable: act out porn fantasies, such as "The Job Applicant," "Taking Dick-tation," or "Do Me or You're Fired." If you don't have your own office, scope out a back stairwell. (Keep your voice down, though: stairwells echo.)

Considerations:

Don't have a quickie in someone else's office, as you're bound to leave a stain, a smell, or something out of place that will be noticed.

On Safari

The sun-kissed plain! The wild beasts running free! What better place to indulge in some animal behavior? Let the pussy hunt begin!

Risk Factor: 3

Having your quickie in view of cheetahs and elephants may stir up your jungle instincts, but safety is always the highest priority when around wild animals. Resist the temptation to do it in the Jeep or tour bus.

DO IT (NOW):

Allow the scenery and heart-racing proximity to powerful, elegant animals to arouse your hunger for your partner. Compare him or her to an animal you see, in terms of strength, swiftness, or beauty. The safari is a time to get dusty, dirty, and sweaty (to say nothing of a good tan). Drink in the sunsets and expansive skies. Once you've soaked all this in, take your quickie to your tent or hut. The safari environment allows for imaginative role-play: the brave hunter and the tourist's wife; Tarzan and Jane; or, more plainly, two lions tearing at each other in a primitive mating dance.

Considerations:

Only feed your animal. And take pictures for your scrapbook.

Opera

Operas are all about love, death, and sex. Why not let the strains of Verdi, Bizet, or Mozart accompany your lovemaking? Besides, unless you're really into it, opera can make you look for something else to think about for three hours. "At these concerts," G. B. Shaw said, "you will find rows of weary people who are there not because they really like classical music but because they think they ought to like it."

Risk Factor: 3

The opera is a pretty public place. Everyone may be looking at the stage, but a lot of movement is going to draw attention quickly if you're in the normal seating part of the concert hall. Being ejected from an auditorium in the middle of an opera with your clothes in disarray is probably an experience you want to avoid.

DO IT (NOW):

The best situation is if you're seated in a private box. You can sit at the back, where the lighting is dim. Time your movements to the music and try to let off any cries of ecstasy during the soprano's aria. If you can't afford a private box, you can always try discreet manual stimulation. A coat on your lap helps conceal any activity from your seat mates. During intermission, you may be able to find a secluded corner of the hall for a quickie, but watch out for wandering opera fans.

Considerations:

Tuxes and ball gowns can be awkward to get in and out of quickly.

Location 106:

Parachuting

What's sex without thrills? And doesn't he say that orgasm is like running up to a cliff and jumping off? Do him one better, and just do him.

Risk Factor: 5

If you're nervous when the condom breaks, imagine how you'll feel if the parachute breaks!

DO IT (NOW):

We suggest having your quickie in the plane before the jump: there's plenty of time for that. Or, after you hit the ground and you're riding high on adrenaline, strip off your parachute (and everything else), and do each other where you land. Logistically, performing intercourse while you're plummeting to earth may be beyond the both of you, although we have heard of nude skydiving. Such a thing may be harder on the gents: I know I wouldn't want my loose equipment flapping around while I'm traveling 80 miles an hour downward.

Considerations:

The only thing worse than your 'chute not opening is discovering that you enjoy the thrill of parachuting more than sex with your partner.

Parade Site

Who doesn't love a parade? The marching bands, the floats, the clowns—and everyone's attention focused on what's coming down Main Street. This leaves you and your partner an opening.

Risk Factor: 5

With the exception of gay pride or political protest parades, you're going to have a lot of kids around. And at all parades, one finds a contingent of police. You don't want them to find you.

DO IT (NOW):

Your best bet is to choose your parade wisely, and the wisest choice is the Mardi Gras parade in New Orleans. Bear in mind that even those folks have a limit of tolerance for naughty behavior in public. Another strategy, if you can't make your way to the Big Easy, is to hold your quickie on a rooftop along the parade route, out of public view. This will give you the thrill of open-air sex, public sex, and having sex serenaded by a high school marching band playing "Louie Louie." Good times.

Considerations:

If you can find a nudist's parade in some European capital, hey, go for it.

Location 108:

Parents' House

Of all the places you're supposed to respect and revere, your parents' house tops the list. These are, after all, the people who brought you into the world, the people who raised you to be the person you are today. But when they're out for a drive on a Sunday afternoon, find some thrills on their bed.

Risk Factor: 1

As always, timing is everything. As long as you're assured you'll have the house to yourselves for some time, you're not going to have any problems.

DO IT (NOW):

Don't be too obvious about wanting your folks out of the house. Suggest something they enjoy doing together and explain that the two of you are too tired to accompany them. You'll just sit here in the living room and relax with a couple of nice books and magazines. Of course, as soon as the car pulls out of the driveway, make your way upstairs to the bedrooms. When you're finished, check to make sure everything's back the way it was. No rumpled comforter, no blankets knocked on the floor, no adult videos left in the DVD player.

Considerations:

Bratty younger sister unexpectedly coming home from soccer practice.

Park

Ah, the park! What a lovely spot to go for a stroll, have a picnic, skip stones in the pond, or get both hands down your lover's pants. The French are fond of doing it "en plein air," so give it a whirl.

Risk Factor: 3

Depends on the park. Not all parks have roaming rangers, straying kids, wandering dogs, or some dude asking if you've seen his football anywhere.

DO IT (NOW):

The bigger the park, the better. Remember that in addition to the little park down the street with the swingset, there are state and national parks that are the size of some small towns. These parks afford plenty of room and plenty of hiding spaces. You might also seek out a nudist park or even a private park. A little research and willingness to travel will pay off. The only caveat is, if you go to a large park, don't wander off so far in search of privacy that you can't find your way back to your car. Word to the wise: Bring bug spray, a blanket, heavy boots, and sunscreen. Be prepared.

Considerations:

Your man's suggestion to have sex in a park may take you to a baseball park. Tell him you'll only go to second base.

Party

The conversation is meaningless small talk, the snacks are stale, and they're still pumping foam out of the keg. This party needs a little pick-me-up. So pick someone up.

Risk Factor: 2

People disappear at parties without much difficulty, so you and your partner always have an out by saying you need to refresh your drinks, powder your nose, or have a quickie. (Say that last one out loud only if the music is deafening.)

DO IT (NOW):

Don't hide away in the coatroom, because people need their coats. And don't tie up the bathroom, because if it's a keg party, the beer is likely in the bathtub. Remember, too, that bored party guests like to explore the house and snoop around, telling people they're just admiring the décor. Try the basement. No one in a party ever goes there. Or the attic. You'll return to your party relaxed and ready to propose a game of charades. For your first puzzle, you and your partner can act out, "We just had sex in the hosts' walk-in closet." People will never guess that one.

Considerations:

The phrase "I was drunk" excuses all manner of crass behavior at a party, so work on your slurred speech.

Phone Booth

Yes, there still are phone booths out there, and not just in old Superman comics. Some things need to be private, like a confidential conversation or a dirty conversation that leads straight to your quickie.

Risk Factor: 5

The corner phone booth is made entirely of glass, in case you hadn't noticed. And finding another quarter to keep your call going isn't easy when you cannot find your pants.

DO IT (NOW):

Hotels and fine-dining establishments often have phone booths that are really small rooms with a door that closes. Find one of these, and, if possible, use an overcoat to cover the small window. There should be only one seat in the small room, which the gentleman may use; the lady may sit forward on his lap, if you get me. To make this quickie even hotter, use your phone call to dial a 1-900 phone sex number. When you heatedly tell the person on the other end that you're doing it in a phone booth, who knows? You may get them off, and then they'll owe *you* money.

Considerations:

The phone booth quickie gives new meaning to putting your lover on hold.

Photo Booth

What pair of lovers haven't engaged in the giggly ritual of having your photos taken in a photo booth? Now how about taking your lover in a photo booth?

Risk Factor: 5

It's not uncommon for two people to crowd into the photo booth to have their picture taken. You've seen two pairs of legs, sticking out from the bottom of the curtain. But if your pants happen to be around your ankles, you will draw suspicion.

DO IT (NOW):

Despite the cramped quarters, you may be able to pull off a few shots of breast sucking or cock yanking. It all happens so quickly! Pose, click. Pose, click. Suck, click. Before you insert your money, come to a decision as to what poses you're going to strike and get appropriately undressed. If you've got the hots and the cash, slip in another bill and go for another set of snapshots. This could get expensive, but some thrills are worth it.

Considerations:

If anyone outside the photo booth tells you to get a room, tell them that this is the smallest room you could get.

Location 113:

Piano

We bet Frederic Chopin stopped in the middle of composing a few times to get it on with Georges Sand. In fact, that might be what makes his music so romantic. Whether they actually did it on Chopin's piano or not is anyone's guess, but it wouldn't be surprising if they had.

Risk Factor: 1

As long as you're using a baby grand piano (more about this below), you should be fine. Even falling off won't do any permanent damage. The biggest risk is probably to the piano, but some sacrifices are necessary in the name of art.

DO IT (NOW):

An upright piano is right out as a possible location. You need a grand, with the lid closed to provide some room. Since the fine surface scratches easily, take off all your clothes before getting up onto it. A bit of Lemon Pledge afterward should remove any unsightly marks and stains. It would be a bit inconvenient to have someone actually playing the piano while you're on top of it, but you might put on some piano music as background.

Considerations:

Possibly having to get the piano retuned afterward.

Pickup Truck

You're looking to turn your pickup truck into a hook-up truck, and when they say the bed is "ram tough," now you know why. Don't those shock absorbers need testing? A little quickie will put 'em through their paces.

Risk Factor: 1

The pickup truck is basically a bed on wheels, which means you can drive it or park it in a place of supreme privacy. You don't even have to leave your garage! Turn on the battery, crank up some tunes, and spread out on the bed!

DO IT (NOW):

Safe bet here is to put some throw pillows or an old mattress in the bed of your truck. Cold metal on your ass doesn't rank very high for turn-ons. Car-sex tunes are a welcome touch: e.g., "Like a Rock" by Bob Seger, or "I Can't Drive 55" by Sammy Hagar. Having sex in your motor vehicle is a way of christening it with good luck, and for safety's sake, you might want to bless the bed of your pickup truck once a month, just for maintenance.

Considerations:

If you have a quickie in your boyfriend's or husband's pickup truck, tell him part of the deal is that he may not thereafter refer to it as the "fuck truck."

Picnic Table

Who doesn't enjoy a nice spread on a picnic table? The summer heat, a powerful thirst, and the invigorating air of the outdoors has you and your partner looking around for the nearest thing to a bed.

Risk Factor: 2

Depends on where this picnic table is. A newly installed table in a pristine park is good, while a termite-infested table tucked in a sap-soaked corner of a rest stop is . . . well, not so good.

DO IT (NOW):

Always a good idea to pack a tablecloth in the car. This makes for clean eating and safer fucking. Plus, the red-and-white-checkered background is a wholesome contrast to your dirty deeds. Ensuring that you have privacy, make liberal use of finger food as foreplay. Slip a pickle into your lover's mouth. Feed him a generous helping of potato salad. Ask if he's up for seconds, or thirds. If the picnic table has a bench attached, put it to use in your varying positions. Oh, and keep napkins nearby.

Considerations:

If you're near the woods, you may have a bear watching from a distance, shaking his head and saying, "Animals . . ."

Planetarium

There's nothing like exposure to some heavenly bodies to give you a sense of perspective as to your place in the universe and what life is really all about—getting some, for example.

Risk Factor: 3

As long as you are not seated next to a Girl Scout troop or a visiting elementary school science class, you should be in good shape, getting naughty in your seat. Everyone's neck is craned upward, and it's dark.

DO IT (NOW):

Use the planetarium lecture to begin your foreplay. Discreetly drape your coats over your laps, and imagine what it would be like, up there in the stars, all alone with your partner, two desperately lonely astronauts. Once you skip out, explore the planetarium for hideaway spots. I'm thinking behind the model of Jupiter, since it's so big (I mean the planet, silly). If you can sneak into the behind-glass display of the moon surface, you might come upon (or come in) a roomy crater. Space is all about exploration, so trek around to find a spot where your man has boldly gone before and is dying to go again.

Considerations:

Even one small step can mean a giant leap for your relationship.

Police Station

If something has gone wrong with one of the other locations listed in this book, it's possible you and your partner may find yourself in a police station. Some people find police uniforms a wild turn-on, no matter what the circumstances. In any case, if you're going to be cited anyway, why not go a little further?

Risk Factor: 4

Chances of your being alone and unobserved at a police station are not very good. And if you're caught, there are plenty of people around to explain the laws of public indecency to you. A lot of discretion is called for here.

DO IT (NOW):

Speed is of the essence. With luck and some distraction (possibly another prisoner being brought in or a sudden announcement by one of the police captains), you might be able to slip into a closet. You won't have long at all before you're missed, and you've got to get out of your hiding place before there's a general search. Plan on about two minutes maximum of enjoyment time before zipping things back up, pulling things back down, and slipping into the main room of the station. If anyone asks where you went, you can say, "Oh, just to the restroom. Didn't I tell you I was going?" If you're lucky, that may work.

Considerations:

SWAT teams responding to an emergency.

Political Rally

Okay, you showed up, you made your presence known, you sent a message to Washington, whatever. Now what? While other people are calling to get out the vote, you and your partner will be getting out your goods for a feel-good quickie.

Risk Factor: 5

If you're present at a supercharged political rally, on an issue of national importance, chances are excellent that the place is crawling with police, undercover detectives, Secret Service, and, worst of all, bloggers with cell phone cameras waiting to catch something controversial.

DO IT (NOW):

Your best bet here is to engage in some political theater. One idea is to put on a puppet show, with hand puppets acting out how The Man is oppressing the people. As with all overtly political entertainments, feel free to give the public something truly awful and heavy-handed, while out of sight, you and your paramour engage in libidinous exercises. Another idea is to hold a "love-in" as a retro form of protest. Face it, they can't arrest all of you.

Considerations:

Political rallies attract all sorts of nuts. Take advantage of the opportunity to dress scantily or in a costume that hides your partner from view.

Pool Table

Under the glowing overhead lamp, you sink your last ball and turn to your partner. Now's the time to claim your prize for winning the match. No need to go upstairs to the bedroom when there's an inviting green surface waiting for you.

Risk Factor: 0

Assuming, of course, that the pool table is in the privacy of your own home, about the only difficulty you'll face is in not tearing or staining the felt. If you're in a pool hall, of course, that's a different story.

DO IT (NOW):

Remove your shoes before getting up on the table. Otherwise you may tear the surface. The table under the felt is extremely hard, so your best bet to avoid some painful bruises is for the man to be on his back with the woman straddling (and being careful not to bang her knees against the table). For foreplay, try rolling a ball gently along your partner's skin; the smooth, flawless surface can be a real turn-on.

Considerations:

Getting the table surface level again.

Location 120:

Public Fountain

You and your partner have each tossed a coin into the fountain to make a wish, and something in your eyes suggests that you've got the same thing on the mind. Make your wishes come true!

Risk Factor: 5

Amorous couples sitting fountain-side don't excite controversy or censure; couples engaging in a quickie are another matter. Once again, it's that whole quibbling issue about "no sex in public." Gol, whatevs!

DO IT (NOW):

Public fountains offer a 360-degree view, so there's no rear side to hide behind. There also may not be enough statuary to conceal your quickie. Solution? Public fountains tend to shut down for autumn and winter. Depending on their size, the fountains may be covered with tarpaulin: if they are not, show up with your own—plenty of it. Enlist your man's construction skills to erect a tarpaulin-covered section of the fountain so any passersby will think it's under repair. For added security, hit the fountain at night.

Considerations:

If you run from the police, you are going to leave behind a trail of wet footprints.

Location 121:

Public Restroom

Getting your quickie on in a restroom may sound cliché, but having a quickie in a dozen weird places that don't include a restroom is more suspect than having a quickie in a restroom and nowhere else.

Risk Factor: 4

The variable here is the location of the restroom. Is there high traffic? Are there doors on the stalls? Does it smell like French perfume or fresh stink? Choose wisely.

DO IT (NOW):

The upscale restaurant in the middle of the afternoon will have a clean, sweet-smelling restroom that's practically abandoned. If you elect the men's room, pick a stall and get into position: ladies straddling their men while standing up. This way, anyone who comes in will see only two male feet at the bottom of the stall. The women's room presents a more formidable challenge, because no matter the time of day, there's always a line. The women will wonder what a guy is doing taking up a valuable slot in the queue.

Considerations:

Ladies, if you are discovered coming out of the bathroom stall with your man, have your man pretend he is blind, and help him wash his hands. Tell confused onlookers that the restaurant doesn't allow seeing-eye dogs.

Public Swimming Pool

It's summer. You and your significant other are poolside, surrounded on all sides by families, lifeguards, and oblivious sunbathers. The sun beats down, you start sweating and decide that not only is it time to take a dip, it's time to get busy.

Risk Factor: 2

This situation doesn't present much in the way of physical danger (nothing worse than the bugs you could pick up from swimming in a public pool to begin with); however, you could get thrown out or, worst case, arrested for public indecency.

DO IT (NOW):

Here's the best way to get away with the deed. Leaning up against the side of the pool is far too obvious, and sure to announce your intentions throughout the pool. Instead, try the following. The man carries the woman, her arms around his neck, legs wrapped around his waist. Loose fitting swim trunks and a surreptitiously moved aside thong provide easy access for the fun parts. The male then simply walks across the pool, carrying his girl (who weighs only a fraction of her normal weight in water). The walking motion provides the enjoyable stimulation you need without making it obvious what's happening.

Considerations:

Curious kids with dive masks.

Pumpkin Patch

Remember Charlie Brown, Linus, and the Great Pumpkin? Really, when you think about it there's something sensuous about pumpkins. They're big, and round, and . . . orange. On a dark night, pick out a comfortable spot and find a new way to greet the Great Pumpkin.

Risk Factor: 2

Apart from stray dogs or other animals wandering around, a pumpkin patch at night is a pretty deserted place. You'll probably have the privacy you want, and if you bring along a nice thick blanket, you're not likely to have any scrapes, prickles, or bruises either.

DO IT (NOW):

For just the right atmosphere, the best night is Halloween. By dark, children and their parents will be roaming the streets in search of tricks and treats, and you can have some peace and quiet to do what you want. The middle of the patch is best, and the leaves under the blanket can make a nice, soft mattress. If you're lucky and the patch is away from any houses, you don't have to be especially quiet; some howls and squeals can add to the atmosphere. Since this is the end of October, though, only partial disrobement is recommended, and a bottle of wine to warm up afterwards is a nice accompaniment.

Considerations:

Squashed, rotten pumpkins.

Rafting

Danger and sex go together (remember James Bond?) and doing it while whitewater rafting is likely to satisfy both urges. Imagine yourself in a deep canyon, with tall, cool walls, and the sun burning down overhead. Somewhere ahead of you, you can hear the distant roar of rapids as you slip out of your clothing and move toward one another.

Risk Factor: 4

Sex in most boats, except a yacht or an ocean liner, presents challenges. But in this case, there's timing to be considered. Trying to have sex while going through rapids isn't advised. You'll both be out of the raft and into rough water in no time at all.

DO IT (NOW):

Choose a moment when the raft is in calm water and isn't likely to be carried away by a dangerous current. Give yourself some time before you're likely to hit any rough patches of swift-moving water. If you're rafting in a canyon, you'll probably be wearing helmets, which you shouldn't remove. The same applies to life jackets. Swimsuits are optional. It's probably best that both of you lie down to provide some measure of stability to the raft. Keep a sharp ear for approaching rapids and be prepared to sit up, grab your paddles, and paddle like hell.

Considerations:

Tourists with cameras; other, faster rafters approaching from behind.

Location 125:

Recumbent Bicycle

Turns out there really is a way to make these things cool.

Risk Factor: 5

Back when you were a kid, you may have ridden on your friend's bike's handlebars. Dangerous, but not extremely so. Trying to have sex on any kind of bike while going up or down a hill is like trying to do your taxes on a roller coaster. One thing at a time, stud.

DO IT (NOW):

Any bicycle or athletic equipment store should carry (or can order) a stationary bike stand, which allows you to pedal indoors in a stable position. Outfit your recumbent bicycle with one of these, and you and your lover strip to your sneakers. Traction is important for you both. Gents, enjoy the "cowgirl" position here. Man your bike, and let your lady straddle your saddle. Pedaling while she's pounding may not be feasible, but you're more interested here in stability than in spinning your wheels. Best of all, there is no need to wear those dorky helmets we all have to wear now (unless, of course, that turns you on).

Considerations:

If you deflate, ask your lover to blow you up.

Restaurant

Ever since the banquet scene in *Tom Jones*, we've associated food with sex. A restaurant is a great place for exploring one another. Not only are you having sex—it's catered. Start with some champagne and oysters to set the right mood and finish with a rich, dark chocolate mousse.

Risk Factor: 3

Restaurant staff aren't very tolerant of people having sex at the table. On the other hand, the chef may take it as something of a compliment to the aphrodisiacal power of his cooking.

DO IT (NOW):

High-end restaurants provide the most opportunities. Ask for a table near the back, but not too near the kitchen, since there's a lot of traffic in and out of those doors. The best situation is one in which the lighting is low and your table is separated from others by walls or curtains. Plan things for right after the appetizer is served; that should give you a little enjoyment time before the waiter shows up with the entrees. To be really daring, crawl under the table and service your partner while the waiter is pouring additional wine into your glasses. As long as the tablecloth reaches almost to the floor, you'll be safe from discovery.

Considerations:

Plan to leave the waiter a bigger tip than usual for his discretion.

Location 127:

Rest Stop

Every experienced driver knows that "box lunch on the highway" refers to a quickie in a rest stop. If you're nodding off at the wheel, take a break and get your heart racing! Pull over and take off that pullover.

Risk Factor: 5

Guess what: You're not the first person with this idea! State troopers and other police, undercover and otherwise, routinely patrol rest stops for shenanigans of all kinds—public sex topping the list. You don't want to get swept up in a dragnet.

DO IT (NOW):

Park behind an 18-wheeler, in an unlit corner of the rest stop, or behind the fast food restaurant. Making your quickie stop some time other than broad daylight also works in your favor. Putting your car's "sunshield" up and draping your jackets from a crack in the windows ensures more privacy. For role-play foreplay, one of you could be The Grateful Hitchhiker or The Lonely Visitors Bureau Desk Attendant. Don't head into the woods; that's where teams of perverts gather.

Considerations:

If you're an elected official, avoid holding illicit sexual encounters here. Taxpayers won't appreciate you using rest stops for your private adventures.

Rocking Chair

The soothing, gentle back-and-forth motion, so relaxing and comforting. And then there is the pleasure of sitting in a rocking chair.

Risk Factor: 2

Depending on how rough you like it, there's always the chance that you will rock so hard in either direction that the chair will capsize, taking you and your lover with it. Try explaining this to the insurance company.

DO IT (NOW):

As with most chair scenarios, the gentleman is seated with the lady on top and facing the other direction. A few starting rocks will reveal that while the rocking chair moves you and your partner forward and back, it's rather hard for, ahem, you to rock forward and back at the same time. So, keeping the chair steady and still, rock your lover: then, ease forward and back to rock the chair. Get a steady, satisfying rhythm going and, as stated above, go easy.

Considerations:

While you're getting it on in the rocking chair, what is Grandma supposed to do? Crochet standing up? You rascally young'uns!

Rodeo

Ready for a bucking good time? Itchin' to "cowboy up" into the cowgirl position? Rarin' to swing your partner? Okay, you get the point.

Risk Factor: 1

They called it the "Wild West" for good reason, and good ol' boys and gals are no strangers to a good ol' time. Still, rodeos are like circuses in that they can attract the whole clan, so be wary of wandering kids.

DO IT (NOW):

The rodeo offers a wide variety of activities that can serve as foreplay for you and your partner: roping and tying, square dancing, line dancing, mechanical bulls, and maybe even pie eating contests. At some point during the evening, you must encourage your partner to let out a vigorous "yeeee-hah!" of approval at one of the rodeo's offerings, because this is a terrific turn-on if you make it throaty and strong. (It's rehearsal for later.) Note the presence of empty horse trailers and changing rooms for rodeo clowns. Take full advantage of them.

Considerations:

Gals, when dressing for a quickie, sport a skirt with no undies. Just make sure you keep a pair in your purse, in case your guy wants to give you a twirl on the dance floor.

Location 130:

Roof

Ah, lying out under the stars on a summer's evening. The air is warm, there's not a cloud in the sky, and the only sound is the gentle chirping of the crickets below you. You're away from the world with the one you love. What better time for fun?

Risk Factor: 4

Unless you've got a flat roof (which takes away some of the thrill and is really cheating a bit) you'll need to be careful that you don't roll too far in your enthusiasm. You have privacy but not a lot of stability.

DO IT (NOW):

Especially if your house is some distance away from your neighbors, you shouldn't have to worry about being caught. Even if you are, you're on your own property, so there's nothing much they can do about it. The real issue is ensuring that you don't fall off the roof. The woman should lie, feet pointing down toward the eaves, while the man lies on top of her. Other positions such as kneeling, straddling, or the more complex moves of the Kama Sutra aren't recommended. As long as your heads are pointing toward the ridge line of the roof, you should be safe with some room for vigorous movements.

Considerations:

Swooping owls and unexpected rain showers.

Rowboat

You're lying entwined, drifting on a summer's day. The sky above you is azure and cloudless, and in the distance you can hear the gentle quacking of ducks. Slip out of your clothes and let yourselves go.

Risk Factor: 1

Rowboats are pretty steady, but there's a decent chance of taking on water if your weight is distributed too far to one side or the other. Enough rocking and you might even tip the craft over.

DO IT (NOW):

Both for the sake of safety and for maximum concealment, you should both be lying down. Any attempt to sit up suddenly, and you risk disaster. Choose a spot well away from the shore in a placid lake or pond. Take your time. A rowboat isn't the place for violent, lustful sex. You'll enjoy it more if you let the gentle rocking of the craft set your rhythm. You can prop the paddles up against one of the seats to be out of the way. Just don't make any sudden or violent moves. It's best if you concentrate on moving your hips rather than your whole body, since that'll create the least wobbling.

Considerations:

Curious boaters, wondering at the sight of an apparently empty rowboat.

Scuba Diving

Muff diving is all well and good, but unless you and your partner are in an orgy, you can't do it at the same time. Scuba diving, on the other hand, is a more accommodating pleasure.

Risk Factor: 5

Making love in an environment with no natural oxygen supply entails risk. Problems with equipment and position can lead to panic, which leads to Davy Jones's Locker. Not good.

DO IT (NOW):

Remember that you do not have an indefinite oxygen supply, so get right to it. Don't be distracted by the awe-inspiring beauty of the barrier reef. First, wear bathing suits: diving suits aren't made for easy-access nookie. Second, don't remove flippers for toe-sucking. Third, opt for the "cowgirl" position of woman on top, as this allows for intercourse with the least amount of equipment obstruction.

Considerations:

While scuba diving may be fabulous for a fuck, it's not the time or place for fucking around. If you're having difficulty or encountering problems, it's safety first.

Location 133:

Secondhand Store

Your local consignment or secondhand store saves you the trouble of driving all around town and having quickies at yard sales. It's one-stop shopping when you're feeling cheap. Real cheap.

Risk Factor: 2

Let's just say that secondhand stores cannot depend on an exclusively high-class clientele, so the arrival of freaks and social deviants won't surprise anyone.

DO IT (NOW):

Make sure your secondhand store has a good-sized clothing section and changing rooms. Remember, too, that the salespeople are also struggling to make ends meet, so greasing their palms will help you in greasing your lover without interruption. The fun part about clothes shopping here is that you can use the clothing as costumes and engage in some role-play in the changing room: the gentleman can be the discharged soldier in that used military jacket, and the lady can be his honey at home in that 1950s-era polka-dot dress.

Considerations:

If you're discovered by a fellow shopper or salesperson, ask them if they want to lend a second hand in your secondhand sex.

Shower

In these times of conservation, it's a good idea to save water. Combining two showers into one is a good way to "green" your sex life— giving pleasure while doing good. Not only that, you'll be clean when you come out.

Risk Factor: 1

The shower doesn't have too many hazards, and if one of you slips, the other's there to catch you. And you're in your own home, so there are no issues of privacy involved.

DO IT (NOW):

You'll both be standing, but there are a lot of positions to try. If you're feeling daring and have the muscles for it, the man can lift the woman against the side of the shower while she wraps her legs around his hips. Another possible position has the woman facing the wall while the man enters from behind. The water should be of a temperature you both feel comfortable with. There's nothing more deflating than trying to make love when you're scalding hot or freezing cold.

Considerations:

Stray soap cakes.

Skiing

Skiing and sex: full of twists and turns and the excitement of speed, both activities are recreation at its best. Gliding over a sheet of water or snow will gear you up for a slide through the sheets.

Risk Factor: 1

Why so low a rating? Well, we're not about to suggest that you have sex *while* you're skiing. That requires a level of daredevil acrobatics best left to your fantasy world.

DO IT (NOW):

Learning to ski on snow is the ultimate winter foreplay: keep your legs apart, crouch down, and then fall over and roll around with your partner. The ski lodge was built so that horny skiers can take it inside and warm up. If you're water-skiing, you'll inevitably fall into the water, giving your partner the opportunity to rescue you and administer mouth-to-mouth, even if you don't need it. Remember, too, that cross-country skiing is an activity so athletically rigorous, you'll want to conserve some energy for when you shed your layers..

Considerations:

Having sex with your snow skis or water skis still on is one interesting challenge. If you pull it off, you've earned major bragging rights.

Location 136:

Sledding

You're squeezed close together on a tiny little sled, holding on for dear life as you cascade down the hill. Around the time you can no longer feel your hands or feet, you start to feel something else.

Risk Factor: 4

Frostbite isn't fun, especially in the nether regions. It's best for the seated person to keep his or her pants on to avoid naked glissading, which can be rough on the bum.

DO IT (NOW):

Toboggans make for the most convenient type of sled to do the deed on given their length. However, just about any sled will work. If you're on a sled that is made for only one person, have the man sit upright and the girl straddle him, wrapping her legs tightly around his waist (snow boots come in handy in case the feet drag in a moment of release).

Done discreetly enough, it will just look like two people facing each other and hugging while whizzing down the hill. And remember, screaming is a socially accepted noise for sledders to make, so no need to mask your pleasure cry.

Considerations:

Watch for flying (snow) balls.

Sleigh Ride

When you jingle all the way, you really jingle all the way! The horse knows the way to carry the sleigh, so sit back, relax, and keep warm with a quickie to match the horse's quickstep. O what fun!

Risk Factor: **2**

Sleigh rides typically take place along a wooded trail, and your driver has his or her back turned, so you're relatively safe for a lay on a sleigh.

DO IT (NOW):

That heavy blanket across your laps is your best friend. The guy remains seated with the lady sitting atop him, facing him, and the blanket discreetly draped to shelter exposed body parts from the cold. The sleigh in motion will provide a natural rhythm and jostle, and the bracing cold air will stimulate your senses. Over the hills you'll go, laughing (or moaning) all the way. If full-blown coitus is out of the question, the blanket provides perfect cover for oral sex, but ask your driver to announce any sharp bumps on the trail beforehand. Enjoy some hot cocoa afterwards, although you'll be sufficiently warmed up already.

Considerations:

Shared body temperature is the best way to keep warm in the cold, and hands get warmed up fast when inserted into your lover's lap.

Location 138:

Smart Car

As Smart Cars are becoming more popular in this country, it's inevitable that people are going to find other uses for them. The smallness of the car, which doesn't have a backseat, presents some challenges, but it also gives you greater intimacy both when you're driving and when you're . . . not.

Risk Factor: 3

Even though there are lots of ways to ensure privacy, the small size of a Smart Car guarantees that you're going to stick yourself or your partner with a gear shift knob or the steering wheel. So you may have to put up with a few bumps and bruises in the cause of experimentation.

DO IT (NOW):

If your Smart Car is in a public place, you won't have much privacy; it's not as if there's a back seat you can get down in and stay out of sight. The best bet is to find a secluded place in which to park. If the man stretches his legs across both seats and the woman sits on top, you should have just enough room to maneuver. Try to avoid knocking against the emergency brake, particularly if you're parked on a hill.

Considerations:

Environmental enthusiasts who want to examine your car.

Stage

You can't get much more public than a stage. That's where people go, after all, in order to be seen. But if you can find a dark, empty theater, with only a single spotlight shining on the middle of the proscenium . . . it's magic.

Risk Factor: 1

As long as the theater is deserted and locked and you've got the keys, you're safe. If you're not supposed to be there and someone spots you and calls the police, things could turn out badly, but a quick dash through the fire exit will preserve your anonymity.

DO IT (NOW):

It works a lot easier if one of you is an actor with a gig in the theater. Then, at least, you've got an excuse for being there. A prop couch or bed can make for a perfect setting, though it might be a bit on the lumpy side. For some extra fun, borrow some of the costumes and have a little fun role-playing before you undress each other. The theater is magic. However, if, when you finish, you hear applause coming from the audience, it might be a good idea to hightail it out of there.

Considerations:

The ghost of Norma Desmond.

Steam Room

Is there anything that relaxes you more after a good workout than a steam? The answer is Yes: another workout. Have this workout during the steam, and your body (as well as your lover) will thank you.

Risk Factor: 4

People with heart conditions and respiratory ailments might want to think twice before having sex in the intense wet heat. It's like running in place, in a hot tub.

DO IT (NOW):

Naturally, you'll want privacy. Steam doesn't provide the same cover as a heavy fog, and you're not fooling anyone by holding up your towel while your lover goes down on you. The key here is to take it slow. If basic foreplay brings you to orgasm, quit while you're ahead: you don't want to overdo it (or overdo your partner). Bring some massage oil into the steam room and give your partner a helping hand. Rub, enjoy, relax, and let yourself get heated. If you've got the stamina and endurance, go for it. The whole experience will really open up your pores.

Considerations:

If you decide not to go for it, you're going to come out of the steam room looking like you had a quickie anyway.

Strip Club

Think this one will be easy, huh? Lots of naked and horny people around, so no problem, right? Wrong! This is the hardest place of ALL to have your quickie!

Risk Factor: Nuclear

Strip clubs exist as a way of using partial nudity, simulated sex, and a full bar to soak men of their money. Period. With severe enforcement that would make you shudder, strip club owners most definitely don't want you having sex in their joint. It could mean the loss of their license, and that'd make some people very, very angry.

DO IT (NOW):

Don't go for the obvious places: the "champagne room," the strippers' dressing room, the manager's office (because he's already having sex in there himself). And doing it on the stage is the stuff of fantasy. Your best bets here are: (1) Climb onto the roof of the strip club and have sex there; (2) Get a job as a stripper and have sex in the manager's office; (3) Open up your own strip club and have sex with the strippers; or (4) Join the police department and start dating a stripper.

Considerations:

Use your cell phone to take a photo, because no one is going to believe you did it in a strip club.

Subway

Subways used to be dirty, noisy, hot, and dangerous. They're still noisy. But with the dirt and danger down, you can make a subway car hot in a whole new way. So descend into the tunnels and make some sex in the city.

Risk Factor: 3

Apart from the chances of getting caught in such a public place, there's always the danger of being robbed—though this is less on most subways than it was thirty years ago. Stations themselves are probably inadvisable. They're damp, dirty, and you want to stay well away from the tracks to avoid falling.

DO IT (NOW):

The easiest situation is if you're either alone in the car or with very few people. Choose seats all the way at the other end of the car, facing away from everyone else. The woman discreetly lifts her skirt while the man lowers his pants just enough to get at the vital bits. The woman sits on his lap and lets the train's vibrations help in the stimulation. It's best to choose to do things between stations that are quite a distance apart. The last thing you want to happen is a crowd of teenagers to pour onto the train while you're still engaged.

Considerations:

Wandering transit police.

Supply Closet

This one has almost obtained the status of a classic. For anyone wanting some quick, private sex on the job, the supply closet offers the most possibilities. Surrounded by mops, brooms, and the smell of disinfectant, forget about what's going on outside and concentrate on each other.

Risk Factor: 2

Supply closets are filled with, well . . . supplies. Thus it's easy to bang into something, knock something over, or trip over something. In any case, unless you're careful, noise and consequent discovery is a big factor.

DO IT (NOW):

Assuming you're in an office environment, it's best to choose a time when traffic in the hallway will be at a minimum—say, lunchtime. Most supply closets are small and cramped, so you'll be standing up. If possible, move as much of the miscellany to one side of the closet, giving you some room to work with. Keep most of your clothes on, since if you're found out you don't want to stand in the hallway struggling to pull on your pants or skirt.

Considerations:

That blasted janitor.

Swing Set

You decide you want to take a trip down memory lane after running into your elementary school crush at a bar so you head to the local playground.

Risk Factor: 3

Be careful not to get too much air while swinging. If you think falling on the woodchips hurt when you were five, try it now half-clothed. Not fun. You also risk getting arrested if you're in a park after dark.

DO IT (NOW):

If you ever did the "spider" with another person on a swing when you were younger then you already know how to start this. Have the man sit down on the swing and the woman (wearing a skirt) straddle him with her legs coming out the other side of the swing. You should resemble a four-legged spider, hence the name. Then, all you need to do is start pumping your legs in turn to get some air. The pumping motion is all you need to get busy on the swing.

Considerations:

For added danger level, try this on the swing set in your neighbor's backyard.

Taxi

When it's too far to walk and you feel like conserving your leg strength for other activities, it's time to hail a taxi, which, if you play your cards correctly, is a big yellow mattress on wheels.

Risk Factor: 2

Here's all that taxi drivers care about: (1) You pay; and (2) You don't throw up in the taxi. Other than that, what you do in their back seat is your business. The two things you should care about are: (1) a curious driver not keeping his eyes on the road; and (2) potholes, if you're giving your man oral.

DO IT (NOW):

The magic words here are telling the driver ahead of time what your plans are. Don't be oblique or coy: Tell your driver you're interested in a long enough ride to have sex in his taxi. Before he protests, flash a hundred-dollar bill and tell him not to put the meter on. That's dough straight into his pocket. Also assure him that you won't make a mess or leave stains on his back seat. If he goes for it, remind him to find a smooth route and only to speed up and swerve on your request.

Considerations:

If you get held up in traffic, remain low.

Tent

Most red-blooded men wake up in the morning pitching a tent with their blankets, if you know what I mean. Why not take your quickie to a real tent?

Risk Factor: 3

If you can stick your hand out of your tent and touch the tent next to you, you're too close. Make sure you have privacy.

DO IT (NOW):

The beauty about a tent is that you can pitch it indoors as well as outdoors. If your partner isn't entirely on board for sleeping outdoors, pitch the tent in your living room and have a party. Show your partner how much fun it can be, snuggling in a sleeping bag. Feed each other s'mores. And remember the Scout motto of always being prepared, so bring protection. The next step is to take the tent into the backyard. Then the state park! Then the Grand Canyon! (Funny: it always looks the same, when you're inside the tent.)

Considerations:

Remember to build your campfire outside the tent. Shared body warmth inside the tent will keep you plenty hot.

Terrace

A terrace allows you the homey convenience of taking indoor activities outdoors: cooking, cocktails, journal writing, quickies, quickies with cocktails. You've got the space, why not use it?

Risk Factor: 2

Doing it on the terrace poses no dangers: it's a question of privacy. Rooftop terraces are good options, as the only folks who can look down on you are in the sky.

DO IT (NOW):

Make it romantic. Break out the outdoor candles, fire up the grill, dress in a loose-fitting sundress, and set the mood for a long, relaxing evening at home—relaxing, of course, until you start snogging and dare to go all the way. Just as food tastes better on the grill, sex feels better outdoors, and on the safety of your terrace you don't have to worry about the hard dirt floor or being crammed into the backseat of your car. If you have company, take "entertaining guests" to a new level. Perhaps your hospitality will extend from "My house is your house" to "My spouse is your spouse." Who knows what'll happen when you start to relax?

Considerations:

Be sure your spouse knows what you mean when you suggest you "eat outdoors" tonight.

Toilet

If a woman rules the roost in a house, the bathroom is the nicest room under the roof. It's a woman's sanctuary, her pleasure dome. (Hint to guys: Clean the bathroom as foreplay.) Sex here has its pleasures.

Risk Factor: 1

If the door locks, you're safe from intruders. Just remember that many household accidents take place in the bathroom (slippery tub floor, all those razors, extreme exfoliation).

DO IT (NOW):

Get naked. Now you and your partner are ready for foreplay in the tub or shower. Heavy soaping is encouraged. Men need to know that shampooing a woman's hair and massaging her scalp is a form of safe sex. After some mutual toweling and lubrication, show the gentleman why it's always a good idea to leave the seat down. With him in a sitting position, sit on his lap and get sweaty all over again, requiring a second cleansing. Make generous but judicious use of body balms, powders, and perfumes. Follow up a pedicure with toe sucking. No need to keep it clean.

Considerations:

Be careful not to drop any electric sex toys into a water-filled tub.

Toll Booth

Late one night, you're on a toll road and you discover too late that you're out of change. You don't have your E-ZPass, either! It's a good thing you're EZ, so you can bribe the toll taker.

Risk Factor: 3

Toll takers have monotonous and pretty undemanding jobs, but doing nothing but making change all day is a sweet deal if you can swing it. Prey on their boredom and tempt them with your discretion. This may be the easiest 50 cents you ever saved yourself.

DO IT (NOW):

Ladies, open your blouses as you pull up to the booth and explain that you've looked and looked and you're plumb out of change. You would, however, be willing to barter for your toll, provided you can pull over and squeeze into the booth. Kneeling down and giving the toll taker "one for the road" should be more than enough to pay for each axle of your car. Heck, you may even get an E-ZPass out of it. Focus on out-of-the-way toll booths and unpopular exits. The toll taker will have a night to remember, and may even tip you with a token.

Considerations:

Be sure to wash your hands afterward. Who knows where all those coins have been?

Location 150:

Tool Shed

Lady Chatterley got it on with her gardener. Maybe there's something about spades, potting soil, and lawnmowers. In any case, in the spring when the air is full of growing things, the tool shed offers a lot of exciting possibilities.

Risk Factor: 4

Privacy isn't an issue; sharp, pointy things are. The tool shed is full of, well, tools. Just be sure not to impale yourself on anything and you should be fine. It's also probably as well to avoid overturning sacks of manure.

DO IT (NOW):

Since the interior of the tool shed isn't likely to have light, be sure to bring along a flashlight. Sometimes you can find some burlap sacking. If not, bring along an old blanket, one you don't mind getting dirty. If you're not worried about the neighbors peeking in, leave the door open. Midday is a good time, since it will be warm and comfortable. Think about trying it just after mowing the lawn, when you smell of new-cut grass and sweat is running down your chest. Be as loud as you like. You can always tell anyone who hears you that you were testing your new chainsaw.

Considerations:

Particularly avoid trimming shears.

Location 151:

Trailer

Think of a trailer as a bed on wheels. And don't even think of having your quickie in a trailer that's stationary! No, no, my friends: Hook up your trailer and hook up on the road!

Risk Factor: 0

When you're speeding down the highway in your trailer, no one's going to be knocking at your door. And with all the blinds and shades drawn, feel free to party and make as much noise as you want.

DO IT (NOW):

Attach your trailer to a motor vehicle, yours or a friend's, and enlist them to take you for a spin on the highway. (Promise to return the favor, once you've changed the sheets.) Then hit the highway. You and your lover will be feeling the earth move beneath you, because you'll be having sex at 70 miles an hour. Go ahead, scream, holler, wail, and cry out! No one can hear you on the road, and the driver has the radio on too loud.

Considerations:

If your ride gets pulled over for speeding, don't have the trailer rocking or the state trooper will come a-knocking.

Train

If holding your quickie onboard a train sounds like a challenge, here's what you do: just keep repeating to yourself, "I think I can! I think I can! I think I can! Oh God! Right there! Yes! Yes!"

Risk Factor: 3

Depends on the train: sleeper train, commuter train, or amusement park train.

DO IT (NOW):

You best bet on the commuter train is to head all the way to the rear car where the bathrooms are: no one wants to sit there. Remember to wait for the conductor to punch your ticket before you punch your lover's. For optimal privacy, get a ticket for the sleeper train. The space may be a little cramped, but this creates intimacy. If you dare to do it while you're in your seat, ask the conductor for a blanket (or bring your own), and cover up your and your lover's laps while you "give each other a hand."

Considerations:

In the heat of passion, watch your hands: the last thing you want to do is reach up and pull on the cord for an emergency stop.

Tree

When Joyce Kilmer wrote that he'd never seen a poem lovely as a tree, he might not have been thinking of its potential to support sex. Still, a tree can be a fun place to experiment if you have a good sense of balance, no particular fear of heights, and a creative imagination.

Risk Factor: 3

The higher you go, the higher the danger rating should get. If you can stay fairly close to the ground, even falling shouldn't hurt that much, but there's a risk of broken bones no matter what.

DO IT (NOW):

If possible, choose a tree in your own backyard, well away from the eyes of prying neighbors and children. The ideal tree should have large low branches, broad or sufficiently close together that you can lie on them and hold on to them. The man can sit facing the woman, who wraps her legs around him while at the same time holding on to branches over her head to provide support. He holds on to her waist while moving. As long as the branch doesn't break or a windstorm doesn't come up, you're fine.

Considerations:

Inquisitive squirrels and nesting birds.

Tree House

Every couple needs to get out of the house once in a while, and a tree house allows you to not go far. Toss aside the sign that reads "No Boys Allowed" or "Girl Hater's Club." It's time to climb!

Risk Factor: 1

Your only risk here is making too much noise, so keep it down to birdlike squawking and monkey sounds. Squirrels will appreciate your shaking nuts loose from the tree, and your lover will appreciate your shaking his nuts.

DO IT (NOW):

The current vogue in tree houses is custom-made cottages that have the square footage of a studio apartment in Manhattan, so privacy's not an issue. Remember that you're paying for a hideaway, reading spot, and meditation center, all in your backyard. Ensure that the roof is leakproof, in case you want to be outside during that rainstorm, and keep things clean of critters and their detritus. If any nosy neighbors complain about suspicious noises, always say it was turkey vultures. Turkey vultures hang around in trees and are the ugliest birds on earth, so they are an easy scapegoat.

Considerations:

Calling your tree house hideaway your "fuck hut" takes away some of the romance.

Location 155:

Tunnel

You can't get more sexually suggestive than a train or car entering a tunnel. (Okay, the phallic Washington Monument comes close.) Speeding into a long dark passageway? Sounds like my prom night.

Risk Factor: 3

You're either going to walk into a tunnel to have your quickie or have the quickie while you're in a vehicle of some kind: both are risky. And no matter how new the tunnel is, there's always the fear that it'll cave in on you. Maybe that enhances the thrill for you, maybe not.

DO IT (NOW):

Your safest bet here is a railroad tunnel. Not only are they long (the Cascade Tunnel in Washington state is 2.6 miles), but being aboard a train means you don't have to worry about driving during your quickie. Wherever you hold your train quickie—in the heat of the engine room or the privacy of your sleeper car cabin—see if you can start and complete your quickie during the tunnel passage. Intense foreplay can speed things along. With the right moves, you and your partner will see the light at the end of the tunnel, and it will be white-hot.

Considerations:

Conductors nagging you for your ticket while you're busy trying to unhook a bra or open button-fly jeans.

Under the Bleachers

It's not just for the jock and the cheerleader. Under the bleachers, where the grass is soft, the air is warm, and there's the roar of the crowd at a home game, it's the perfect place for you to score.

Risk Factor: 2

Provided no one else has the same idea, there's not much reason for someone to look under the bleachers. As long as you're reasonably discreet, you won't want privacy. There's not much physical danger, aside from the possibility of mud.

DO IT (NOW):

Move to the back of the area, as far away as possible from the crowd. This will reduce your chances of being seen. Football games are noisy, so a bit of extra hollering won't matter. Lying down, standing, or kneeling—it's your choice. You certainly don't want to be out of your clothes on a cold fall evening, so pick a time when the weather's still warmish and you can lose most of your clothing. A blanket's always a good idea to provide a cushion and, if necessary, cover.

Considerations:

Spilled soft drinks from above.

Video Arcade

Give a gameboy the ride of his life, or help a gamegirl reach a new high score. You'll never get so much from a simple deposit in a slot.

Risk Factor: 4

You run two risks here: (1) getting kicked out by the manager, if he or she is actually on the premises; and (2) being so distracted by sex that your Pac-Man gets eaten, your combat fighter gets his heart torn out, or your motorcycle veers off the ski jump and into the sea monster's mouth.

DO IT (NOW):

Home gaming has reduced the number of video arcades in the world, but there are still a few around, and you may find you can rent out the whole place under the pretext of throwing a birthday party. Again, depending on surveillance, you may be able to get away with a quickie amidst all that noisy bleeping and blooping. Look for the driving rides that have a semi-enclosed area you can sit down in. Guys, start your engines and playfully invite your lady to try the game while sitting on your lap. Hopefully, she is used to driving stick.

Considerations:

Gamers (and sex addicts in video arcades) are highly prone to repetitive stress disorder.

Vineyard

A tour of a local vineyard is a lovely way to spend an afternoon with your loved one: beautiful scenery, aromatic surroundings, and enough free wine to drown a yak.

Risk Factor: 3

Depends on how big the vineyard is. If you're in California or France, you and your lover may wander off, hand in hand, into the vineyard and never be heard from again. If the "vineyard" is the trellis over your Uncle Luigi's driveway, you're in less luck.

DO IT (NOW):

Find a huge vineyard and visit during slow hours. With an inviolate air of pretension that no one dares challenge, inform the vineyard keepers that you and your lover are taking a stroll to "inspect the vines." Emphasize that you need privacy in order for your nose to function keenly. Once you are comfortably hidden among the rows of grapes, try pouring that Riesling over your lover's naked chest and lick it off: offer a judgment on its "finish." Ladies, inspect your lover's grapes for tenderness, ripeness, and "mouthfeel." Remember that lovers age well like fine wine, and that you may need to squeeze a few grapes to produce a good vintage.

Considerations:

Clear your palate afterward.

Walk-In Freezer

If you're looking for some privacy for a quickie, look for a spot where no one loiters. A walk-in freezer in a restaurant fits the bill—but you'll have to make this quick.

Risk Factor: 5

You know what happens when you put your tongue on a flagpole in winter? 'Nuff said. Keep bare flesh to a minimum, and not just for warmth. Cold has a way of hitting your extremities first, so dress appropriately.

DO IT (NOW):

There are several ways in (I mean, into the freezer). You could arrive at the restaurant posing as health inspectors, insisting you not be disturbed as you check for nasty stuff like mice. You could also pay off the head waiter: tell people you're considering opening your own place and you're just having a little look-see. In this scenario, you'll want to arrive well before dinner hours, because the mad rush will ensure that the prep cook needs entree to the freezer. Finally, you could pose as repairmen and say that in order to obtain an accurate reading for the freezer temperature, you and your partner need to be inside with the door closed for at least four minutes.

Considerations:

If you have room in your pants, take a brisket for later.

Location 160:

Waterfall

Displays of Nature's might and majesty—storms, volcanoes, the Grand Canyon—have a way of inspiring people, either to write a poem, contemplate their place in the universe, or say, "Hey, what if we screwed in front of this?"

Risk Factor: 3

No one's going to kick you out of a waterfall. Your real danger here is positioning yourself so that you are not directly under thousands of pounds of falling water. That will put a damper on your quickie.

DO IT (NOW):

Bear in mind that not all waterfalls are big enough to provide ablutions to King Kong. Going au naturel in a waterfall and you'll almost surely enjoy privacy, safe access, and water temperature that makes your nipples as hard as radio dials. To be safe, wear shoes with traction on the soles: you don't want to slip and hit your head (or other body part) on a rock. Having your quickie beside rushing water instead of in the middle of it has its pleasures, too, so do what feels safe.

Considerations:

Did I mention that water can be extremely cold?

Waterslide

Sailing down a waterslide, in the middle of physical love, combines the thrill of speed with extreme lubrication. Such a potent combination of childlike and adult pleasures should be illegal, but fortunately, it's not (yet).

Risk Factor: 4

As with regular sex, your pain and discomfort will depend on how well lubed you are. Too dry, and you're prone to skid marks and burns. Too wet, and keeping your bodies interlocked will prove impossible. It's worth trying again and again.

DO IT (NOW):

Some water parks will allow you to go on a slide with a partner, but I don't know of any (even in Las Vegas) that would assent to your request to assume the missionary position before sliding down. So for simpler fun, set up a water slide in your backyard. Be sure that the slide has a hefty weight tolerance. An alternative to sliding down together is for your partner to position himself or herself at one end, while you slide down and aim for the target. You may get a bruise or two, but you're sure to get a lot of laughs.

Considerations:

Consider taping this one. Naked lovers on a waterslide has viral video potential. Overlay sound effects of screeching cars.

Water Tower

Tap into your inner teenager and scale the local water tower. Any idiot can spray-paint "Zep Rules" on its outside, but the quickie is reserved for the truly daring.

Risk Factor: 5

Local police are on the lookout for juvenile delinquents and taggers scaling the water tower, and the mere fact that you're up there ensures a trespassing charge. Sex adds potential charges of indecent exposure, public fornication, and intent to cause a breach of public morality.

DO IT (NOW):

Nighttime is the best time. Wear black. Also wear black on the outside. Consider painting your faces black: should you get caught, no one is going to think you're a cat burglar, trying to rob a water tower. Make your ascent and lay low while you lay. Once you're done, take in the view and get out of there. Should the police be waiting for you at the bottom of the ladder, simply nod confidently and tell them you are a two-person public citizen patrol, making sure there are no kids out late on a school night, causing mischief.

Considerations:

Resist the temptation to spray-paint the water tower with something like, "Joey and Donna Done It Here."

Location 163:

Wedding

Everyone thinks about sex at weddings—and not just the bride and groom. Amid the gowns, the tuxes, the rice, and the wedding cake, sneak off into a back room with someone for a little fun and games.

Risk Factor: 1

Let's face it—even if you're caught, you probably won't get in trouble (unless you're having sex with the bride or groom). And you can always explain that you were caught up in the moment and felt particularly romantic after seeing the happy couple united at the altar.

DO IT (NOW):

Before or after the ceremony is best; during is a bit on the tacky side. After the wedding, when everyone is milling around, kissing the bride, you probably won't be missed for a little while. Find a room away from the action. If possible, one with a lock on the door. If one of you has participated in the wedding, try to avoid rumpling your clothes and hair too much, since that'll probably raise some eyebrows when you rejoin the crowd. The room to avoid is the one where the wedding presents are stacked, since some people may be trying to add their gifts to the pile.

Considerations:

Wandering flower girl/ring bearer.

Location 164:

Winery

In vino veritas. In wine is truth. Of course, in wine is also sex. Wine has been easing the way for sexual pleasure since sometime a couple thousand years ago when people discovered that drinking fermented grape juice made them feel pretty good. Surrounded by the intoxicating smell of Chateauneuf-du-Pape, let yourselves float away on a dark, dreamy river.

Risk Factor: 2

Wineries don't, on the whole, encourage sex on the premises, but even if you're caught you can chalk it up to the effects of the wine you sampled. Who knows? The tour guide may be impressed that the wine was that effective.

DO IT (NOW):

These days most small wineries run regular tours, together with tastings. If you time things right, you should be able to lag behind the main group and find a quiet corner. You'll have to be quick, since if you're gone too long you'll be missed and the tour guide may come back to make sure you haven't fallen into one of the fermenting vats. When you catch up to the others, take a couple of quick sips of wine and comment how it's so good that it's made your cheeks flush. Your fellow tourists may believe you—or not.

Considerations:

Other tourists to whom the wine has imbued with the same idea.

Woods

You're taking a nice hiking trip through the woods with your lover. You've never noticed it before, but there are some very convenient and hidden places to get down and dirty. Suddenly, being a nature lover has never felt so naughty.

Risk Factor: 1

Unless there are a lot of people hiking trails, the danger level is low on this one. Just don't get caught by a park ranger. Watch out for poison ivy or poison sumac. You'll get itchy in places you never knew existed and explaining the situation to your doctor might be embarrassing.

DO IT (NOW):

If you are in the woods on private property or in your own backyard, you won't have to be that careful. If there are other people in the area you'll need to find a private spot. A cluster of large rocks can provide the privacy you need and give you something to lean against if you don't want to do it on the ground. If you were prepared and brought a blanket you'll be protected from bugs, dirt, and poisonous plants. If you bring a second blanket you can drape it over yourselves and keep hidden from any spying hikers.

Considerations:

People bird watching with binoculars. You might not know they are watching because they don't have to be close.

Location 166:

Zoo

How did Cole Porter put it?

The chimpanzees in the zoos do it.

Some courageous kangaroos do it.

So why not take a leaf from the animals' book and release your own inner critter? When the tiger starts to roar, do a bit of roaring of your own.

Risk Factor: 2

If you're careful not to get caught, there's not much danger in a zoo—provided you stay out of the cages. On the other hand, there are going to be tons of children around, so discretion is the better part of valor.

DO IT (NOW):

Thirty or forty years ago, zoos were mostly big "houses" where the animals were kept in small cages. Today's zoos have a more open, free-flowing design, which offers more opportunities for enjoyment . . . of every kind. Find a clump of bushes or a small grove of trees. It's probably best to stay clear of the main attractions; you don't want to be interrupted by a group of tourists eager to see the zoo's new pandas. Standing is going to provide the most opportunities. Lying down, you'll find it harder to make a quick getaway in the event of discovery.

Considerations:

Foreign tourists with cameras.

About the Author

Kate Stevens is a professional writer and editor who believes in making love, not excuses. Of all the places she and her lover have had sex, her favorite is a rest stop on Cape Cod, Massachusetts, in broad summer daylight: she was in the driver's seat, her back to the windshield. Kate and her partner live and love in Rhode Island.

Acknowledgments

Special thanks go out to the following for lending their creative muscle to this book: Andrea Norville, Peter Archer, Judy Bernardi, Jacquinn Williams, Kat Schroeder, and Spiro Serimentez.

Getting Where Women Really Belong

- Trying to lose the losers you've been dating?
- Striving to find the time to be a doting mother, dedicated employee, and still be a hot piece of you-know-what in the bedroom?
- Been in a comfortable relationship that's becoming, well, too comfortable?

Don't despair! Visit the Jane on Top blog—your new source for information (and commiseration) on all things relationships, sex, and the juggling act that is being a modern gal.